THE

·Basic·Basics·

WINE
HANDBOOK

THE
·Basic·Basics·

WINE HANDBOOK

RICHARD KITOWSKI
AND
JOCELYN KLEMM

GRUB STREET · LONDON

This edition published in 2003 by
Grub Street
The Basement
10 Chivalry Road
London
SW11 1HT
Email: food@grubstreet.co.uk
www.grubstreet.co.uk

British Library Cataloguing in Publication Data
Kitowski, Richard
The basic basics wine handbook
  1. Wine and wine making
  I. Title II. Klemm, Jocelyn
  641.2'2

ISBN 1 904010 54 7

First published in Canada as *Clueless About Wine* by Key Porter Books
Typeset by Pearl Graphics, Hemel Hempstead
Printed and bound by Biddles Ltd, Guildford and King's Lynn

CONTENTS

DEDICATION

To our families for your love, patience, and support during the writing of this book and our journey with wine. We're sure we drive you crazy when we go on and on about wine, but you never show it. Thank you for allowing us to indulge our passion.

ACKNOWLEDGEMENTS

Thanks to Clare McKeon for your enthusiasm to make this project grow and bear fruit, and to Monica Meehan for planting the seed. Our gratitude goes also to Teresa McArthur, Raymond Kitowski, and Valerie Toth for your helpful advice and thoughtful comments on the manuscript during the fermentation process. To Laurie Coulter, special thanks for crafting and refining our words before they were bottled. And thanks to the many people we've talked to while writing this book that encouraged us along the way.

To all of you we raise a glass of wine.

THE OPENING

READY TO POP THE CORK?

"Let's see, is it white wine with white meat, red wine with red meat? My boss is having salmon, our client is a vegetarian, and I'm ordering pork! And I'm expected to pick the wine! What do I choose?"

Like the person in this imaginary situation, you too may have come to realise that you are clueless about wine. Relax, you are not alone. In fact, you are actually in the majority. Probably less than 3% of the world's population knows a lot about wine.

Most wine books and magazines seem to be written for people with some wine knowledge, or assume the reader is already a professional wine taster. That's where we come in. We wrote *The Basic Basics Wine Handbook* to take the mystery out of wine and replace the intimidation factor with knowledge and enjoyment. Wine shops and sommeliers don't have the monopoly on wine knowledge; everyone can learn about wine. It isn't that difficult.

This book is packed with practical information, from the basics about how wine is made, to where it's made and what it should taste like, to which wine goes with which food. We'll also talk about what to buy, how to entertain with wine, how to keep wine, and even how to give it away. We've included a four-step programme to help you taste wine like a professional. So turn the page, maybe pour yourself a glass of whatever wine you have, and get ready to learn the secrets of wine.

ICONS

This symbol points to food and wine matching suggestions.

This symbol – a bottle of red wine crossed with a white wine – indicates versatile wines that work with a variety of foods or cuisines.

The tastevin is a symbol associated with a sommelier – a specialized wine professional whose job it is to make your experience in a restaurant a memorable one. It indicates advice, suggestions, or general tips about wine.

WHAT IS WINE, ANYWAY?

A BASIC SURVIVAL KIT

Perhaps you don't give much thought to the wine you drink. As long as you like how it tastes, what it cost, and how well it goes with what you're eating, what more do you need to know? After all, do you need to know how an engine works to drive a car?

With wine, reputation and quality and many other factors affect the price you pay. It's worth your while to know a little about what goes into the bottle, in the same way that knowing a little about mechanics may save you money when you're having your car repaired.

But talking about winemaking and grapes can be boring. It's what you can do with the information that's interesting. So in the following pages we'll give you only the absolute basics of what goes into making a bottle of wine.

IS IT ONLY FERMENTED GRAPE JUICE?

Well, mostly. Wine can be made from hundreds of different fruits and plants (ever had dandelion wine?), but the type we are going to focus on is made from grapes. Check any dictionary and you'll find wine defined as "a beverage made from fermented grape juice." But there's more. Fermentation is how grape juice is converted into wine. We aren't talking about the kind of juice you find on your supermarket shelf, but juice from grapes grown specifically to make wine.

Typically the winemaker adds yeast to the juice, which reacts with the natural sugars in the grapes to produce alcohol. There are a couple of other byproducts – heat and carbon dioxide – which are important in the production of sparkling wines.

The ripeness of the grapes determines their sugar content, which in turn determines the potential alcohol content of the finished wine. Generally speaking, the riper the grapes, the higher the alcohol content. There is a limit, however, as most yeasts die off when the alcohol level reaches about 16%. This is why you will never see a table wine stronger than 16%.

If the grapes don't ripen enough, some countries or regions allow sugar to be added to the grape juice to boost alcohol levels in the finished wine. If you want to impress your friends, this is called *chaptalization*. This practice is the exception, however, not the rule.

No sugar is added to the finished wine itself to make it sweeter. Sometimes if the sugar isn't totally consumed by fermentation, some sugar – called *residual sugar* – is left in the wine, making it taste sweet. Even so-called dry wines have residual sugar, but the levels are low and almost undetectable.

A typical bottle of table wine is made up of 84% water, 12% alcohol, and 4% natural compounds – some 500 by last count. These natural compounds include vitamins, minerals, sugars, and acids that are very important to the taste, smell, and texture of the wine.

Chemistry
Sugar (in the grape juice) + Yeast = Alcohol + CO2 + Heat

Natural Compounds

Alcohol

Water

THEN WHY DOESN'T WINE SMELL LIKE GRAPES?

When we teach our wine classes, often one of the first questions we're asked is, "If wine is made from grapes, then why does it smell like raspberries or vanilla or green peppers and not grapes?" followed by, "What makes one wine smell and taste different from another?" So let's talk about smell and taste for a moment.

Things smell because of the odorous compounds they emit. Wine has about 200 known odorous compounds. They trigger a memory of something else – maybe something fruity, spicy, earthy, or something you can't quite put your finger on. Some wines will remind you of raspberries, others of pineapples. One wine (Sauvignon Blanc) even reminds some people of cat's pee! These compounds tend to be set for each type of wine so once you know how a particular wine smells, you have a good chance of being able to remember it again.

Taste is a bit different. We can taste only four things: sweetness, sourness, bitterness, and saltiness. Since there shouldn't be any discernible taste of salt in wine, that leaves three. Without the sense of smell we can determine only if one wine is more or less acidic, sweet or bitter than another. When we put smell and taste together we have *flavour* – the true taste of a wine.

So if wine is mostly water, why does it taste and smell the way it does? Because of three factors: the grape itself, where it's grown, and how it is made into wine.

Did You Know?
Only one wine grape smells like grapes when made into wine – Muscat. Try Asti from Italy and you'll see what we mean.

WINESPEAK

Acidity – a vital component in wine that gives it freshness and longevity

Aroma – the smells of a wine derived from the grapes themselves

Aromatic – highly scented or fragrant

Balanced – when the key components of fruit, acidity, and tannins are in harmony

Big – full of flavour

Body – the weight or feel of a wine in your mouth – either light, medium, or full

Bouquet – the smells of a wine derived from the fermentation or maturation in the bottle

Chewy – a full-bodied wine with noticeable tannins

Classic – "textbook" example of a wine, a benchmark

Clean – no unusual smells

Complex – a multi-dimensional wine with many layers of aromas and flavours

Crisp – refreshing levels of acidity, usually referring to a white wine

Earthy – rustic aromas or flavours in a wine, suggesting soil or minerals

Elegant – refined or delicate aromas or flavours

Extracted – an abundance of natural compounds (namely pigments, tannins, sugars, and minerals) evident in the wine

Finish – end flavour or aftertaste of a wine once it has been swallowed or spit out, described in terms of length

Flabby – lacking in balancing acidity

Flavour – the overall impact of a wine on your senses

Gamey – pungently musky, meaty aromas

Green – unripe aromas and flavours

Herbaceous – pleasant aromas of grass, leaves, and green vegetables

Intense – powerful aromas and flavours

Jammy – aromas and flavours of cooked or overripe fruits, usually associated with wines from warmer climates

Length – amount of time the wine's flavour lingers in your mouth (short, medium, or long)

Neutral – not distinctive

Oaky – the smell or taste of oak in the wine; associated with vanilla, spicy, or buttery aromas and flavours

Petrol – pungent smell, reminiscent of diesel; common in good quality, mature Riesling wines

Round – balanced and complete; nice mouth feel – nothing out of place

Silky – smooth mouth feel

Simple – a wine lacking in depth or complexity

Soft – a red wine low in tannins or a white wine low in acidity

Spicy – exotic aromas and flavours of spices in the wine (e.g., cinnamon, clove, nutmeg, ginger, or black pepper)

Steely – crisp, with mineral aromas and pure fruit flavours, usually referring to a white wine

Tart – bracing acidity

Terroir – describes the unique expression of the vineyard's soil, site, and microclimate in a wine

Unctuous – intense, oily mouth feel, usually associated with very sweet wines

Varietal – a wine named after the dominant grape variety from which it is made or the characteristics of that grape variety

Vintage – the year of the harvest

Zippy or Zingy – refreshing acidity

WHAT'S IN A GRAPE?

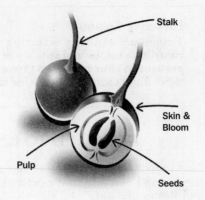

Stalk

Skin & Bloom

Pulp

Seeds

Think of the different varieties of apples that are available at any given time at your local supermarket: Golden Delicious, Gala or Cox's. Each has its own specific colour, smell, and taste. Some are good for eating and others are better for cooking.

Grapes are like that too, and grapes grown specifically for making wine have characteristics that make them stand out from the rest. There are literally thousands of different grape varieties but only a few are used to make most of the wine you drink.

Stalk: contains tannins
Skin: contains colour, tannins, and some flavour compounds
Bloom: the waxy stuff on the skin, contains wild yeasts and bacteria
Pulp: contains water, sugar, acids, and minerals
Seeds: or pips, contain bitter oils

You've probably not thought much about grapes before. You just buy a bunch, wash them, and eat them. Now, we don't know what kinds of table grapes you buy, but we do know that they aren't white or red. Wine grapes aren't white or red, either. White wines are made from light-skinned greenish grapes and red wines are made from darker skinned purplish grapes.

In winemaking, the most important parts of the grape are the skin and the pulp. They contain the key building blocks of wine: sugar, acids, and tannins.

Sugar is converted into alcohol through fermentation. If grapes are picked at perfect ripeness, the desired level of alcohol can be produced.

Acids present in the grapes are transferred to the wine. Acidity keeps a wine fresh as it ages, brings out the fruit flavours, and balances the sugar and the alcohol. A lack of acidity leaves the wine tasting lifeless and "flabby," the way a piece of fruit tastes when it's past its prime.

Tannins play a role in the wine's taste (bitterness) and its fullness (body). They also help the wine age. Grape variety and winemaking technique affect the amount of tannins in the wine.

Fruit

Harmony & Balance

Acidity

Tannin

A wine is considered in balance when these three components are in harmony.

The flavour compounds in the skin and pulp are unique to each grape variety and are primarily responsible for the aromatic qualities of the wine.

Puckering Tannins
Tannins are naturally occurring chemical compounds in grapes that contribute colour and sensory properties to the wine. They react with proteins in your mouth to give a sense of astringency. There are six times more tannins in red wine than in white wine.

DO I NEED TO KNOW GRAPE NAMES?

Not so long ago, wine knowledge meant knowing about a few French regions and maybe about port and sherry. If you knew where Bordeaux and Burgundy were, and that they produced fine wine from Cabernet Sauvignon and Pinot Noir grapes respectively, you were well on your way to being an expert.

Times have changed. France is still a leading wine region but many others are nipping at its heels. And quality wine is now produced from hundreds of different varieties. Today, if you want to know the difference between a Bardolino and a Barbaresco, it helps to know something about the grapes behind the wines.

All grapes grow on vines but there is only one type or genus of vine that is important for winemaking: the genus *Vitis* (VEE-tis). Of the 60 or so species of *Vitis*, classic winemaking grapes come from *Vitis vinifera* (VEE-tis vin-IF-uh-ra), which originated in Europe. Chardonnay, Cabernet Sauvignon, and Pinot Noir are examples of vinifera grapes.

There are several thousand vinifera grapes and each one brings its own aromas and flavours to the bottle. You don't need to learn about all of these grapes, so let's just look at a few of them. Be forewarned, though, not all grapes appear on the wine label under their grape variety name. If the wine is from Europe, more often than not the regional name will have top billing on the label.

THE TOP SEVEN

The first seven grape varieties we're going to talk about – three white and four red wine grapes – are the key varieties. Know these grapes and you know about 75% of the wine made in the world.

The Top Seven can produce simple, inexpensive wines as well as the most expensive. Some are best when enjoyed with food; others are fine on their own. And they're all good fallbacks in case you forget everything else you read in this book.

The ABC Campaign
Due to the worldwide popularity of Chardonnay, and the often boring, dull, and flavourless wine that is produced, the "Anything-But-Chardonnay" (ABC) campaign has become trendy among certain wine writers. While some of this reputation is deserved, it is unfair to paint all regions with the same brush.

Chardonnay (shar-duh-NAY)

"The chameleon grape"
This is the white wine you are guaranteed to see everywhere. Judging by the amount of it in shops and restaurants, many people must think all white wine is Chardonnay.

The grape itself doesn't have much character but is highly adaptable to manipulation in the vineyard and the winery. Chardonnay often receives some kind of oak treatment by the winemaker, sometimes so excessively that you'd think it was actually made from oak, not grapes.

Thankfully, Chardonnay can also be made into a nicely balanced, rich, and intense wine. Wines from cool-climate wine regions, or from wineries where the use of oak is restrained, tend to be the best examples.

Where does Chardonnay come from?

Region on the label	Burgundy (France)
Grape name on the label	United States, Australia, Chile, Languedoc (France), Canada

Which are the very best?	Chablis, Meursault, and Le Montrachet (all in Burgundy)

What should Chardonnay smell like in the glass?

Cool climate (e.g., Chablis)	Citrus, apple, and minerals
Warm climate (e.g., Australia)	Ripe peach, pineapple, and mango

Sauvignon Blanc (SO-veen-YON BLON)

"Zippy and fresh"
When made into wine, this grape is unrestrained, even nervy. It can be aggressively aromatic but it's not for everyone. It appeals to those who like zingy white wines.

Sauvignon Blanc's greatest feature is its high acidity. This makes it a great apéritif wine – much better than Chardonnay, in fact. It can also be made into some very good dessert wine. Winemakers rarely give Sauvignon Blanc any oak treatment. Instead, they highlight its naturally aromatic characteristics. In California, Sauvignon Blanc may be sold under the name Fumé Blanc.

Where does Sauvignon Blanc come from?

Region on the label	Loire and Bordeaux (France)
Grape name on the label	New Zealand, South Africa, Chile, United States

Which are the very best?	Sancerre (Loire) and New Zealand

What should Sauvignon Blanc smell like in the glass?

Cool climate (e.g., Loire)	Gooseberry, citrus (lime), and cut grass
Warm climate (e.g., South Africa)	Citrus (grapefruit), melon, and asparagus

Riesling (REECE-ling)

"Racy and aromatic"

A versatile and food-friendly grape, Riesling isn't as popular as it deserves to be. This is too bad because Riesling is arguably the world's greatest white wine. Try a good version and you'll be convinced.

Riesling can produce crisp, dry, austere wines as well as rich, luscious, sweet dessert ones. In all versions, Riesling tends to be lower in alcohol than most white wines and has very good acidity. And if you're patient, some Riesling wines can age for decades.

Where does Riesling come from?

Grape name on the label	Germany, Alsace (France), Canada, Austria, United States, Australia

Which are the very best?

	Mosel-Saar-Ruwer, Nahe, Pfalz, Rheingau (all in Germany), Alsace (France)

What should Riesling smell like in the glass?

Cool climate (e.g., Germany)	Crisp green apple, citrus (lemon), floral, and mineral
Warm climate (e.g., Australia)	Rich citrus (lime), tropical fruit, peach, and passion fruit

---

LIEBFRAUMILCH

Liebfraumilch (LEEB-frow-milk) was probably responsible for introducing most people to wine. As their tastes change, they desert the familiar medium-sweet style of Blue Nun and Black Tower, yet the association with all German wines remains, severely damaging the German wine industry. Liebfraumilch is actually a blend, primarily of Müller-Thurgau and not Riesling grapes – a fact many German winemakers would like you to know.

Cabernet Sauvignon (CAB-err-nay SO-veen-YON)

"Deep, dark, and aristocratic"

Cabernet Sauvignon (sometimes just called Cabernet) is probably the most famous red wine grape in the world. Although sometimes blended with other grapes, Cabernet Sauvignon can produce wines that can age for decades; its top versions are highly prized by wine collectors.

Although Cabernet Sauvignon's characteristics are recognizable wherever it's grown, it also has the distinction of being able to reflect the unique character of the location in which it was grown. The French call this *terroir*.

Never the lightest wine in the glass, when young, Cabernet Sauvignon wines can be big and tannic – they need time to come around. Be patient and you will get your reward.

Where does Cabernet come from?

Region on the label	Bordeaux (France)

Grape name on the label	United States, Australia, Spain, Italy, Canada, Languedoc (France), Chile, Eastern Europe
Which are the very best?	Pauillac (Bordeaux), Napa Valley (California), Australia

What should Cabernet Sauvignon smell like in the glass?

Cool climate (e.g., Bordeaux)	Blackcurrant (cassis), cedar, and tobacco (cigar box)
Warm climate (e.g., Napa)	Ripe (jammy) blackcurrant, mint, and eucalyptus

---

No Wine before Its Time

As a general rule, the best wines in the best vintages will improve with age. Some examples of wines built for the long haul include German Riesling, Italian Barolo, and French Bordeaux. Most wines (95%), though, shouldn't be kept longer than a few months after purchase.

Merlot (Mare-LOW)

"Soft and plummy"

Like Chardonnay, Merlot is ubiquitous and perhaps overrated. On the other hand, it can make a nice soft, round, and silky easy-drinking wine. Merlot is often a blending grape, adding softness and flavour to its big brother Cabernet Sauvignon in Bordeaux reds. On its own, Merlot is somewhat neutral, but when handled properly in the winery it can produce plump, juicy, almost sweet red wines.

Where does Merlot come from?

Region on the label	Bordeaux (France)
Grape name on the label	Languedoc (France), United States, Chile, Canada, Eastern Europe
Which are the very best?	Pomerol (Bordeaux)

What should Merlot smell like in the glass?

Cool climate (e.g., Pomerol)	Plum, cocoa powder, and mint
Warm climate (e.g., Washington)	Baked cherries, plum compote, chocolate, and mint

Pinot Noir (PEE-no NWAHR)

"Silky and seductive"

While Riesling is the most food-friendly white wine, Pinot Noir (sometimes just called Pinot) holds that distinction for reds. Pinot Noir is also a match for some meats, which Riesling isn't, so it's probably in the number one spot.

Quality Pinot Noir isn't always easy to find, however, as there are a lot of insipid versions out there. "Stick with the best and avoid the rest" is our recommendation. At its best, Pinot Noir is silky and elegant, with good acidity and understated tannins and alcohol.

Where does Pinot Noir come from?

Region on the label	Burgundy (France)
Grape name on the label	California and Oregon, Canada, New Zealand, Australia, Italy
Which are the very best?	Burgundy, Russian River and Carneros (Sonoma, California), Oregon, New Zealand

What should Pinot Noir smell like in the glass?

Cool climate (e.g., New Zealand)	Raspberry, sour cherry, cranberry, and earthy
Warm climate (e.g., Sonoma)	Ripe cherry, raspberry, and smoky

Syrah (see-RAH)

"Bold and spicy"

Are there in fact two names for this grape? While we can blame the Australians for the dual identity – they prefer to use the name **Shiraz** (she-RAHZ) for this noble French grape – you also have to give them credit for bringing the grape back from relative obscurity in the 1980s. Whatever it is called, Syrah is probably the hottest wine grape on the market today.

Heady and aromatic, Syrah is drinkable young (especially the Aussie versions), but its ample acidity and firm tannins help it age for decades. Syrah can also reflect the *terroir* of the region. This is as true in the Rhône – Syrah's ancestral home – as it is in Australia. The choice of name forms the dividing line between the styles: Syrah is deep, austere, earthy, and spicy, while Shiraz is richer, sweeter, and more intense. Like Cabernet Sauvignon, this is not the lightest wine in the glass – the bigger versions need time to come around.

Where does Syrah/Shiraz come from?

Region on the label	Rhône (France)
Grape name on the label	Australia, Argentina, South Africa, Languedoc (France), United States
Which are the very best?	Cornas, Hermitage, and Côte-Rôtie (all in Rhône), Barossa Valley, and Victoria (Australia)

What should Syrah/Shiraz smell like in the glass?

Cool climate (e.g., Rhône)	Blueberries, prunes, bacon, black pepper, violets, leather, smoke, and herbs
Warm climate (e.g., Barossa Valley)	Ripe blackberries, plum, cherry, chocolate, sweet spices, black pepper, and eucalyptus

---

Who's Number 1?

So, what is the most planted grape in the world? Of this group, only Merlot and Cabernet make the top ten. Airén is number one and it's all grown in Spain. It is mainly used to make wine that is then distilled to make brandy.

Quick Identification Chart

The following chart is a cheat sheet for remembering the key words for describing these grapes and where the best wines come from.

Grape	Key Words	Locations
Chardonnay	Creamy, peach, citrus	Burgundy
Sauvignon Blanc	Grassy, gooseberry	Loire and New Zealand
Riesling	Zingy, citrus	Germany
Cabernet Sauvignon	Blackcurrant, cedar	Bordeaux and Australia
Merlot	Plum, leather	Bordeaux
Pinot Noir	Silky, cherry	Burgundy and USA
Syrah/Shiraz	Spicy, blackberry	Rhône and Australia

THE CONTENDERS

The following grape varieties are less well known internationally. On their home turf, however, they do make some interesting and sometimes spectacular wines. Since they make up about 20% of the world's wine production, they're worth knowing, just not in so much detail. If you see one of them advertised or on a wine list, give them a try. We promise you won't be disappointed.

First the white wine grapes:

Albariño (ahl-bar-REE-nyoh) is grown in the Galicia region of Spain and is found in the better versions of Portuguese Vinho Verde. (In Portugal, it is called Alvarinho [ahl-va-REE-nyoh].) It produces light, refreshing, and very aromatic (peaches and apricots) wines that are at their best when consumed young.

Chenin Blanc (SHEH-nin BLON) produces some of the most long-lived white wines in the Loire Valley (France). It's the most planted grape in South Africa, where it's known as Steen. Chenin Blanc has searing acidity and aromas of apple, honey, and almonds.

Garganega (gar-GAN-ega) is the dominant grape in Soave – Italy's leading white wine export. It can produce delicate dry white wines, with aromas of lemon and almonds.

Gewürztraminer (geh-VURTS-trah-MEEN-er) produces in-your-face kinds of wine. These highly aromatic wines – reminiscent of rose petals and lychees – range from full-bodied dry wines to elegant dessert wines. The main growing areas are Alsace (France), Alto Adige (Italy), and Germany.

Grüner Veltliner (GROO-ner felt-LEE-ner) is the most important grape in Austria. It produces wines that are low in acidity with herbaceous and peppery aromas.

Muscadet (mu-scuh-DAY) is mainly grown in the Loire (France). It produces dry, crisp, light-bodied neutral wines.

Muscat (MUSS-kat) is one of the most ancient grape varieties. The four principal versions of the grape produce a number of different styles of wine, from the frothy (Asti) to the dry (Alsace), the sweet (Australian "stickies"), and the fortified (Rhône). The main growing areas are Alsace and Rhône (France), Piedmont (Italy), Greece, Australia, and South Africa.

Pinot Blanc (PEE-no BLON) does well in cool climates, like Alsace (France), where it produces soft wines, with aromas of apple, apricot, and honey. It's called Pinot Bianco in Italy, Klevner in Alsace, and Weissburgunder in Germany.

Pinot Gris (PEE-no GREE) comes in a range of styles and under a host of aliases – Pinot Grigio (PEE-no GREE-jee-oh) in Italy, Tokay-Pinot Gris in Alsace (France). Styles range from the crisp and fresh (Italy) to the spicy, exotic, and full-bodied (Alsace), with aromas of citrus, apples, nuts, and honey. Good Pinot Gris is also produced in Oregon and Eastern Europe.

Prosecco (Pro-SEK-oh) is an Italian grape, primarily grown in the Veneto region, famous for the production of good but inexpensive sparkling wines of the same name.

Sémillon (say-mee-YOHN) in Bordeaux is blended with Sauvignon Blanc to make good dry white wines as well as the world's best sweet wine, Sauternes. It also stands on its own as Australia's famous Hunter Valley Semillon (the Australians drop the accent). A good substitute for Chardonnay, Sémillon has aromas reminiscent of pineapples, peaches, nuts, and honey. It's also grown in California and Washington State.

Trebbiano (treb-ee-AH-no) is a prolific but ordinary Italian grape used in white wine production, including Orvieto and Soave. Under its French synonym, Ugni Blanc (oo-nee BLON), it is the base wine used to make cognac and Armagnac.

Verdicchio (vur-DEE-kee-oh), an Italian grape grown in the Marches region, is famous for its production of excellent lemony crisp dry wines of the same name.

Verdelho (vur-DELL-oh) is the Portuguese grape variety used in the production of Madeira. It was introduced to Australia over a hundred years ago and is now an up-and-coming wine. The best examples have fresh, lime fruit aromas and good acidity.

Viognier (vee-ohn-YAY), a traditional Rhône varietal, is gaining popularity around the world, especially in California. It is exotically aromatic, featuring white peaches, spice, and honeysuckle. Viognier's relatively high alcohol levels make it taste sweeter than it really is. The main growing areas are in the south of France (Rhône and Languedoc-Roussillon), California, and Australia.

And now the red wine grapes:

 Barbera (bar-BEAR-ah), the second most planted grape in Italy (Piedmont), doesn't have the prestige accorded its loftier cousin, Nebbiolo. Barbera produces incredibly mouth-watering red wines that simply cry out for food. They are low in tannins and high in acidity, with aromas of sour cherries, plums, and herbs.

Cabernet Franc (CAB-err-nay FRAHNK) is actually one of the parents of Cabernet Sauvignon (the other is Sauvignon Blanc). Like a parent, it often doesn't get the recognition it deserves. This early-ripening grape produces outstanding wines in the Loire (France), but most of the time it adds acidity and aromatics to the famous blended wines of Bordeaux. On its own, it can exhibit more herbaceous (bell pepper) aromas as well as raspberries and blackberries.

 Dolcetto (doll-CHET-oh) – meaning "the little sweet one" – makes light, dry, uncomplicated, food-friendly wines for everyday drinking. These rustic and earthy wines are low in tannins with aromas of tart cherry, liquorice, and almonds. Grown mainly in Piedmont (Italy), the name of the grape appears on the label alongside the town or area where it is grown.

 Gamay (ga-MAY) is best known under its more famous name Beaujolais. This is the name of a region in southern Burgundy and appears to be the only place in the world where the grape does well. It generally produces light and lively, low-tannin wines with sweetie-like flavours of cherry, strawberry, and raspberry. It is best to treat Gamay like a dry white wine: drink it when you buy it, slightly chilled.

Grenache (gre-NASH) loves the hot temperatures of Spain (where it's called Garnacha) and of the south of France – who wouldn't? It's blended with the Tempranillo grape in Spain to make Rioja and with other grapes in France to make the famous Châteauneuf-du-Pape. In Italy, Grenache is called Cannonau. Australia is producing bold new wines from this grape. Grenache can also be made into an excellent dry rosé wine (France and Spain). Since it appears more often than not in blends, it is hard to pinpoint its aromas and flavours. Generally, it's sweet and spicy with aromas of raspberry and strawberry, and doesn't age too well.

Malbec (mal-BECK) is traditionally used in Bordeaux blends for its colour and tannin. It is also grown in Cahors (France) where it is called Auxerrois. Argentina's best red wines are made from Malbec, and are less tannic and more berry-fruit flavoured than their French counterparts.

Beaujolais Nouveau
On the third Thursday in November, Beaujolais producers race to be the first to release their new vintage of Beaujolais Nouveau. Barely six weeks old, these easy-to-drink wines are usually released to considerable fanfare and ceremony. Bottles are shipped by air to all parts of the world so that restaurants can be the first to serve Beaujolais Nouveau each year. Italy, with its Novello, and Canada also try to get in on the festivities, but there is only one true Beaujolais Nouveau.

Nebbiolo (neh-bee-OH-low) is the grape behind the famous Barolo and Barbaresco wines. These are not beginner's wines; they pack a powerful punch and it can take years for the grip of the tannins to ease up. When they do, however, they can be amongst the most surreal wines you have ever tasted. In the best examples, you'll discover layer upon layer of sweet dark cherries, chocolate, truffles, violets, liquorice, prunes, tar, roses, and cinnamon.

Petite Sirah (peh-TEET see-RAH) – known as Durif in France – produces dark, tannic, savoury wines in California and some bargain-priced wines from Mexico. While its name may suggest otherwise, Petite Sirah isn't related to Syrah.

Pinotage (pee-no-TAJ) is a crossing of Pinot Noir and a grape called Cinsaut and is grown extensively, though decreasingly so, in South Africa. Pinotage produces sweet-smelling, plummy wines but they can be a little bit gamey or rustic – not for everyone.

 Sangiovese (SAN-joh-VAY-zay) is the most planted grape in Italy. You probably know it better as Chianti, the famous red wine of Tuscany. Chianti, another versatile food wine, has mouth-watering acidity and moderate tannins. It offers lovely aromas of sour cherries and herbs tied together with tea-like bitterness and an earthy spiciness. Sangiovese also appears in more heavyweight versions as Brunello di Montalcino and Vino Nobile di Montepulciano, also from Tuscany.

Tempranillo (tem-pruh-NEE-yo) is the workhorse grape behind Spain's ageworthy Rioja and Ribera del Duero red wines. Tempranillo produces lushly textured wines, with aromas of strawberries and blackberries and a spicy, earthy edge.

Zinfandel (zin-fan-DELL) is generally thought to be California's "native" grape. Although experts debate its origins (Italy or Croatia), the wines it produces are definitely Californian all the way. Adaptable, it is used to produce sweet "blush" wines (White Zin), fruity, easy-drinking wines, and even classic, full-bodied wines. The aromas range from bright, juicy cherry and raspberry to deep, lush blackberry, blueberry, and figs.

The contender grapes might be a little harder to locate on supermarket shelves or wine lists. Some of them come from emerging wine regions, are blended with other grapes, or appear under different names on the label. Ask your wine shop to help you find one of these if the description appeals to you. They just might surprise you with something special at a great price.

WHERE IN THE WORLD DO GRAPES COME FROM?

Next to the grape itself, climate is probably the most important factor influencing the smell and taste of wine. After all, it's climate that determines which grapes can grow where and how the grapes develop and ripen.

Cool Climate, Warm Climate

Countries farthest from the equator are said to be *cool climate* wine-growing regions and those closer to the equator are *warm climate*.

Germany is considered a cool climate region, as is New Zealand. While each of these regions receives enough sunshine to ripen the grapes, cooler temperatures keep acid levels in the grapes up. As a result, the wines are lighter bodied, crisper, and less intense than those from warmer climates. Growers prefer early ripening grape varieties in these regions.

The south of France and McLaren Vale in Australia are examples of warm climate regions. Higher temperatures mean riper grapes, but by the time the flavours are at their peak, acid levels in the grapes can drop too low, resulting in an overripe, flabby-tasting wine. Later-ripening grape varieties do better in warmer climates and, on the whole, produce bolder, fuller-bodied wine with higher alcohol content.

Even within a region the climate isn't homogenous. In Burgundy, the climate of the Côte d'Or is different from that of Chablis, only about 90 miles (140 kilometres) further north. While visiting Ghislaine Barthod in Chambolle-Musigny, we learned that adjoining vineyards in the area and even rows within each vineyard have slightly different microclimates. Grapes develop and ripen at different rates according to their specific location within the vineyard. For certain wines – those from Burgundy, for example – the microclimate determines the quality and price of the wine in a given year.

Raising Healthy Grapes

Four main climatic factors influence how grapes develop: sunshine, heat, rainfall, and wind.

DO THEY GROW GRAPES IN BOTSWANA?

Grapes actually grow in two bands around the Earth between latitudes 30° and 50°. There are a few exceptions (Brazil, Peru, Kenya, and parts of the UK and Germany), but generally the locations within these bands have the ideal growing and ripening conditions for wine grapes.

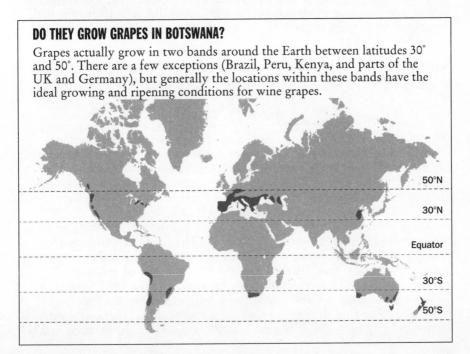

Sunshine – To ripen properly, grapes need a minimum of 1,500 hours of sunshine over the growing season. Red wine grapes need more sun than white wine grapes. That's why you don't often see quality red wines from cool climate regions. Germany, for example, produces more (and better) white wines than red wines.

Heat – If the mean growing season temperature isn't around 60°F (15°C), the vines won't produce. If the temperatures get too high, vines will shut down, and if it's too cold in the winter, the vines will be killed off. Nearby bodies of water – oceans, lakes, or rivers – can moderate temperatures and help grapes ripen in otherwise marginal areas. For example, Napa Valley in California would be too hot to grow grapes if it weren't for the moderating influence of the Pacific Ocean. You will notice on our map that almost all the major wine-growing regions are close to large bodies of water.

Frost is bad. If it hits after the buds have appeared in the spring, it can ruin a harvest. There are a number of expensive ways to reduce the impact of frost but, more often than not, they aren't enough to save the whole vineyard.

Wine in High Places
For every 330 feet (100 metres) above sea level, the temperature drops about 2°F (1°C) and adds a few more weeks onto the ripening period for grapes. This can be a real asset in warm locations like Argentina.

Rainfall – Vines need a minimum of 28 inches (70 centimetres) of water during the growing season. Rain early in the spring is much better than in autumn during harvest. If rain hits at the wrong time, it can burst the berries and create an environment for unwanted diseases. If there is little natural rainfall, some regions allow irrigation, but this is more expensive than Mother Nature.

Wind – Some air movement is beneficial for vines. It can help keep vines dry and free of disease. It can also moderate temperature.

Bad Soil Is Good

Grapes actually grow best in "bad" soil. The more the vines have to struggle to find nutrients, the stronger the vines and the better the grapes. Overly fertile soils encourage too much vegetative growth, which can shade the grapes during the key ripening period. The best soils for vines are porous and drain well (vines don't like wet feet), are moderately acidic, and are good at retaining heat or reflecting sunlight.

There are many different soil types, even within wine-growing regions, and certain grapes do better in certain soils. The Chardonnay grape, for example, is at its best in the chalky soils of Champagne, Chablis, and other parts of Burgundy. Finding the right soil for each type of grape is a science. Prices can be astronomical for the right piece of land. Some wineries go to great lengths – even employing expensive satellite technology – to find the perfect spot for a vineyard. And, yes, you can taste – and pay for – the difference a well-chosen vineyard location makes.

VINE TO WINE

GETTING THE GRAPES INTO THE BOTTLE

Not so long ago, winemakers were pretty well stuck with what was available to them at harvest. Their local wine regulations usually determined what grapes they could grow, and how they should grow them, and they were totally at the mercy of the weather.

Nowadays, with less rigid controls on grape selection, coupled with modern technological advances, it is possible to consistently produce better wine. On the other hand, it is also possible to make Chilean and Australian Chardonnay smell and taste the same – so much so that you'd think there were only three or four winemakers in the whole world. In fact, some of the larger wineries can produce wines to match any style the market desires.

The skill of the winemaker should not be taken lightly. Two wineries, located adjacent to each other, can make wines of different quality from the same fruit grown under the same conditions. Like chefs, some winemakers use their skill and knowledge to create elegant masterpieces while others can make only simple "cookbook" wine.

Whether it is art, skill, science, or the result of deep pockets, let's see how different wines are made and the effect human factors have on the aromas, taste, and quality of a wine.

OUR THREE-MINUTE HISTORY LESSON

When we decided to write this book we promised ourselves we'd be different. We wouldn't bore you with countless details about the history of wine. What we came up with is a three-minute history lesson – the microwave version of 9,000 years of winemaking!

- Millions of years ago, grapes played an important role in the lives of ancient tribes. This little fruit was eaten fresh or dried and could be crushed and drunk as a liquid, though not as wine at this point. Grapes had medicinal qualities and were used for flavouring, tenderizing, and preserving food.
- Early humans discovered that grape juice left in containers fermented naturally, and the result had different flavours and "power." Winemaking was born. The timing is open to discussion, but there is evidence that primitive winemaking was practiced in Asia Minor, south of the Black and Caspian seas. The oldest known pips (seeds) – carbon-dated to between 7000 BC and 5000 BC – of cultivated vines were discovered on Mount Ararat. Further excavations along the southern slopes of the Caucasus Mountains in Armenia, Georgia, and Northern Iran unearthed large clay jars used to make and store wine.

- As early as 3500 BC, Sumerians developed efficient irrigation systems in the barren lands known as Mesopotamia (between the Tigris and Euphrates rivers). Successive civilizations – the Assyrians and Babylonians – showed equal interest in making and trading wine.
- The Egyptians (2800–550 BC) generally drank beer but wine was consumed by the wealthy and in royal circles. The pyramids in the Valley of Kings and Valley of Nobles are decorated with images depicting the grape harvesting and winemaking. Records show the Egyptians understood the negative effects of air on wine as they began to seal their wine vessels with pitch and grease. They were the first to mark these containers with details about the origin of the grapes, the date of harvest, and the name of the winemaker. The first labels!
- The Greeks (2000–350 BC) identified and catalogued grape varieties, invented the pruning knife, recorded winemaking techniques, and developed clay amphorae in which to store wine.
- The seafaring Phoenicians (1400–200 BC) are credited with spreading and propagating vines throughout the Mediterranean Basin.
- The Romans (750–450 BC) further developed grape growing and winemaking practices, including pruning, fertilization, and adding alkaline substances to reduce acidity in the wine. Pliny the Elder, probably the first known "wine writer," classified grapes by colour, time of ripening, and soil preferences. The Romans' most significant contribution, however, was to spread grape growing throughout the Empire: France, Germany, Switzerland, Austria, Hungary, Spain, Portugal, and even England.
- In the Middle Ages (500–1400 AD) the Christian Church, in need of a steady supply of wine for sacramental purposes, slowly started acquiring land needed for grape growing. By the end of the first millennium, it was the largest holder of vineyards. The educated clergy continued to advance the art of making wine. While quantity was the foremost objective of the bacchanalian past, the Church began to be interested in quality. Monks meticulously recorded their results and started to classify wine by variety, vineyard, and vintage.

  For many, wine wasn't a luxury – it was a necessity. Water in most villages and cities was impure, while wine, because of its antiseptic properties, was a much safer alternative. People of all ages consumed it and production focused on getting the highest possible alcohol levels. Countries that could not grow grapes (Norway and Sweden) or whose production was too small to satisfy local demand (England) began to import wine.

- During the Renaissance, wine became a more refined, cultured beverage. As trade in wine flourished, and demand for quality increased, vineyard acreage grew, and new vinification techniques were discovered. The use of bottles and corks and the English invention of the corkscrew made it feasible to keep wine for more than a year, and by the beginning of the eighteenth century, speculative buying (now called wine futures) was established.

  Dom Perignon, a Benedictine monk in charge of his abbey's cellars, established some of the principles of blending the sparkling wine now known as *champagne*. It was actually the English, a few decades earlier, who were credited with the discovery of sparkling wine.

- Colonization brought vines to Africa, Australia, North and South America. In North America, European vines didn't take due to indigenous diseases, but in other countries they flourished.

    Throughout Europe, wine regions experimented with grape varieties to find the right match to the climate and soil. In 1855, the region of Bordeaux developed its famous wine classification system, still in use today, to protect its wine trade.

- Perhaps the single most important event in recent wine history occurred in the mid to late 1800s. Native American grape vines were shipped to Europe for experimental purposes and they carried with them a tiny insect called *Phylloxera vastatrix*. The North American vines had developed a resistance to the insect, but Europe's vines had no resistance whatsoever. First spotted in 1863, within 10 years the insect had spread throughout most of Europe, almost wiping out its vineyards.

    Early attempts to control the insect with pesticides were all unsuccessful. Finally, around 1880, it was thought that since the North American rootstocks were impervious to the insect, grafting European vines onto these rootstocks could solve the problem. This theory proved to be correct, and grafting and cloning are now very much part of modern-day grape growing.

- During the First World War, many of the best vineyards were destroyed. Faced with a renewed demand and low supply, some unscrupulous merchants began selling fake wine. Cheap wine labelled as Bordeaux and Burgundy was actually fermented raisins in water with dangerous chemicals added for colour. The French were the first to fight back by passing laws and regulations guaranteeing authenticity. These policies formed the basis of the first wine production laws.

- In 1919, the Eighteenth Amendment was created prohibiting the sale of alcoholic beverages in the United States. Prohibition ended in 1933 but by that time the American wine industry had been decimated.

- In the past 50 years, world wine consumption has increased substantially. And since 1970, wine production has increased dramatically in Australia, Canada, Chile, New Zealand, and the United States.

    Industry consolidation, combined with an emphasis on global marketing, has produced an unfortunate glut of bland yet fashionable, internationally branded wines – especially Chardonnay and Merlot. The demand for quality wine is increasing, however, and as consumers learn more about wine they are willing to try new things and spend more money.

FROM GRAPES TO THE GLASS

The skills to grow grapes properly and to make wine can be learned through university courses or, as is often the case, acquired on the job.

In the following pages, we will describe the process that takes place at most major wineries. If you ever have an opportunity to visit a winery, take it, as it is definitely the best way to understand and appreciate all that goes into making wine. Besides, most wineries offer free samples, a great way to practice what you learn from this book.

In the Vineyard

Probably the two most important decisions a grower makes is how many grapes to harvest – called yield – and when to harvest them. Vines are prolific: left to their own devices, they will produce literally tons of grapes. They aren't interested in making wine; they just want to produce as many offspring as possible. Grape growers have to control this growth if they want to produce good fruit for winemaking.

If the grower tries to grow lots of grapes per vine, the minerals and nutrients the vine produces are spread out over more grapes. The juice from these grapes will be more dilute and much less flavourful, as will the wine made from it.

Back to Nature

Organic viticulture forbids the use of commercial fertilizers, herbicides, and insecticides. There are no international standards for organic viticulture; however, France and Germany lead the way in terms of local standards. It is hard to tell the difference between organic and non-organic wines from the point of view of taste or quality, so it is a matter of personal choice.

The current trend is toward lower yields. This means cutting away bunches of grapes long before they have developed – called *green harvesting* – to ensure higher quality and more flavourful grapes. The winemaker pays more for these grapes because the grower has fewer of them to sell. In turn, the wine will be more costly to produce.

The South Gets the Jump

In the northern hemisphere the harvest takes place from August to October. In the southern hemisphere grapes are harvested from February to April. Wines from the southern hemisphere have a six-month jump on the north.

Grapes are harvested when the optimum amount of sugar has developed in the grape relative to the acid levels and the particular style of wine the winemaker wants to make. Each grape variety reaches its optimum level at a different time; for example, Pinot Noir ripens earlier than Cabernet Sauvignon.

Brix

Brix is a unit of measurement used to determine sugar levels in grapes. For example, 22° Brix is considered an ideal measure for grapes that will be made into a dry table wine.

Waiting until the sugar–acids balance is just right is no easy task. Pick too early and the grapes may be under-ripe and tart; too late and the grapes may become over-ripe and jammy, or have no varietal character at all. Weather can play a major role in determining when to harvest the grapes. Rain during harvest can dilute the wines or bring on fungal diseases.

When the grapes have ripened properly, or the grower can't wait any longer, the grapes are picked either by hand or by a mechanical harvester and brought to the winery.

In the Winery

The harvested grapes are put into a crusher/destemmer, where they are separated from their stems and leaves and crushed into a pulp called *must*. Before machines, workers merrily stomped the grapes with their bare feet to achieve essentially the same result. In some regions, winemakers still believe that the human foot is better suited for this process than a harsh machine.

The must is then pumped directly to a press for white wine, or to a tank for red wine. The juice in almost all grapes is clear, so the colour of a wine comes entirely from the grape skins. White wine must is pressed immediately so no colour is extracted from the skins. Red wine must is allowed to steep on the grape skins (*macerate*) for days, even weeks, to extract the amount of colour and tannins the winemaker wants.

In the press, juice is squeezed from the must. Care is taken to make sure the must isn't pressed too much; otherwise the juice will become cloudy and astringent. The best juice – called "free-run" juice – runs off before the pressing begins and is often kept separate from the pressed juice.

The juice is then fermented. Fermentation can take place in any type of vat or vessel depending on the flavour desired. Many white wines are fermented in stainless steel tanks, while red wines may be put into oak barrels. Sometimes a combination of both is used. The temperature of the fermenting juice is monitored and sometimes controlled. When the temperature is too low, yeast cells won't multiply sufficiently and fermentation is slow to start. On the other hand, if it is too warm, the fermentation may stop altogether and unwanted aromas may develop in the wine. Modern wineries have temperature-controlled tanks to make sure the desired temperature is maintained.

When fermentation stops, the wine – yes, it can be called wine now – is moved or *racked* to another vessel to mature. Racking removes the wine from as much of the grape solids and spent yeast cells (or *lees*) that collect on the bottom of the vessel as possible. As with fermentation, the wine can mature in a non-reactive or inert tank or in oak barrels.

COSTLY BARRELS

Contrary to the romantic image of wines ageing in a cellar, not all wines are put into barrels. Since a new French oak barrel can easily cost hundreds of pounds, their use adds to the cost of the wine, which the winemakers must try to recover in the price.

Barrels allow the wine to develop unique flavours by providing contact with the air and the wood itself. By allowing some evaporation, they also concentrate the wine. The type of wood used (commonly oak) and the age of the barrels impart other aromatic compounds to the wine and change the wine's texture. The amount of time a wine is left in the barrel also adds to the complexity of the wine.

Depending on the amount of time the wine needs to mature or age, further racking may be necessary to clarify the wine. More expensive wines may be racked several times over the two to three years the wine is in the barrel. Clarifying agents may be used to speed the process but care must be taken not to strip the wine of its qualities. Some red wines receive no clarification at all; that's why you may find some sediment in the bottle.

Once the winemaker has decided the wine is ready to sell, it is blended with other wines or sent directly to the bottling line. Bottling may be done manually, in the case of small producers, or on computer-controlled bottling lines at large commercial wineries.

Despite this oversimplification, making wine is a complex interaction of natural and human elements. It can be as much art as it is science. The result can be beautiful and surreal; or it can be simply a nice bottle of cheap plonk!

In the Bottle

Glassmaking has been around since the time of the Egyptians and the Phoenicians, but glass was too fragile and expensive to use for wine storage until the 16th century. Before that wine drinkers could afford to buy wine only in clay containers (amphorae) or leather bags (wine skins). The corkscrew wasn't invented until the 17th century, so bottles as we know them weren't very practical until then.

Nowadays, wine bottles come in all shapes and sizes. Producers use the label and bottle to make their wine stand out on a shelf and to make a statement about their wine.

How Many Grapes in a Bottle?
It takes the juice of 200 to 300 grapes (about 3 pounds or 1.4 kilograms of grapes) to make a 750 ml bottle of wine.

Bottle shapes

Although some wines are packaged in designer bottles, most of the wine we drink comes in standard bottles. The shape of the bottle can provide clues as to what's inside and where it's from. Local laws require some of the styles, while others are used by tradition. Châteauneuf-du-Pape wines always have the Pope's emblem on the bottle, while the Gattinara bottle (from Italy) often has a handmade look to it.

Standard wine bottles come in five major styles:

- The **bocksbeutel** may be the style you are least likely to see on the shelf – that is, unless you're familiar with Mateus Rosé from Portugal. This short, squat green bottle is also used in Franconia (Germany).

- The **flûte** is the tall, slim green or brown bottle that we all associate with German wines. By law in Alsace, producers must bottle their wines in the flûte-style bottle.

- The most common bottles you will come across are **Bordeaux** style and **Burgundy** style. The Bordeaux-style bottle has pronounced "shoulders" with parallel sides. The Burgundy-style version has sloping shoulders, tapering down to a broader base.
  Now, if life were simple, you would find Bordeaux and Bordeaux-style wines (Sauvignon Blanc, Cabernet Sauvignon, and Merlot) in Bordeaux-style bottles, and Burgundy and Burgundy-style wines (Chardonnay and Pinot Noir) in Burgundy-style bottles. In reality, this holds true only for wines from Bordeaux and Burgundy. By law, producers in these regions must use the approved style of packaging. So the red and white wines of Bordeaux, including sweet wines, are packaged in bottles with shoulders. And the red and white wines of Burgundy are packaged in the bottles with the sloping sides. The Loire and Rhône wines tend to be in the Burgundy-style bottles.
- The **champagne** bottle is a variation on the Burgundy style, but it's made with thicker glass, has an even broader base, and the famous punt in the bottom allows the server to safely hold the bottle in a horizontal position while pouring.

Increasingly, traditionalists are bringing back the bottle shapes used by their ancestors. This could be a marketing ploy but it is also an indication of the intent of the producer to shun modern winemaking practices. And outside of the Old World, any wine can be put in any bottle – it's up to the producer to decide. Always check the label.

Bottle sizes
Bottle capacities range from as little as 100 ml to 15,000 ml (equivalent to 20 standard bottles), but the standard bottle size is 750 ml. This is roughly comparable to the first wine bottles in the 16th and 17th centuries. The size of these early bottles was thought to be a function of the lung capacity of a typical glassblower. The round shape has changed, however, to make it easier to store the bottle on its side.
  Since the demand is low, only a small percentage of the wines produced are packaged in alternatives to the standard bottle. The most common option is the magnum (1,500 ml), which is double the standard capacity. Here are the other bottle sizes:

- Jeroboam   3,000 ml (4 bottles)
- Rehoboam   4,500 ml (6 bottles)
- Methuselah   6,000 ml (8 bottles)
- Salmanazar   9,000 ml (12 bottles)
- Balthazar   12,000 ml (16 bottles)
- Nebuchadnezzar   15,000 ml (20 bottles)

Bottle colour
You may have noticed that nearly all wine is packaged in light green, dark green, or dark brown bottles. The tint protects what's inside from one of its natural enemies – light.

Exposure to sunlight and fluorescent light is very bad for wine. When you see wine packaged in a clear bottle, usually it's to show off what's inside, say the colour of a rosé wine. If the wine is expensive, like a rosé champagne, it will be wrapped in ultraviolet-resistant orange wrap. Not so for a rosé table wine. It's meant to be bought and consumed, and has little risk of seeing much light in its lifetime.

Some wine regions require bottles to be a certain colour. In Germany, for example, a green flûte bottle is used for wines from the Mosel, and a brown flûte for wines of the Rhine regions. Some producers also use colour, design, and even the style of glass to make the wine package part of their marketing plan. For example, Vernaccia (from Italy) often comes in a green-tinted amphora-shaped bottle, and Black Tower (from Germany) comes in a distinctive ceramic bottle so you will always be able to identify these wines quickly on a shelf.

Wine in a Box

Wine is now being packaged in plastic bottles and even Tetra Pak™ cartons like juice boxes. For convenience, wine is also sold in a "bag-in-a-box" container – essentially a plastic foil bag of wine inside a cardboard box. These range in size from 3 to 15 litres suitable for large parties. Since the bag is usually filled without air and the spigot is airtight, the contents can last much longer than bottled wine when opened. The quality of the wine isn't always the highest, but the price is probably right.

A WINE IS A WINE IS A WINE?

SORTING THROUGH THE SHELVES

Thousands of different wines are available on the market today. Some of the range and selection comes from the grape variety – for example, many bottles of wine are labelled *Pinot Noir*. But that's only part of the explanation. Pinot Noir is used to make red Burgundy, it's part of the blend in champagne, and is now even used to make icewine in Canada. Three different types of wines (still, sparkling, and dessert) and the only thing they have in common is the grape!

It isn't necessary to memorize the names of thousands of wines, but it helps to break them down into manageable categories. We've picked five that you're probably already familiar with: still (a.k.a. table wine), sparkling, fortified, dessert, and aromatized.

STILL WINE

This is the wine you most likely drink on a regular basis. Some people call it *table* wine. Most wines in this category fall between 8% and 15% alcohol by volume, and much of it is close to the middle of that range, around 12%. German wine laws allow wine to be as low as 6.5% alcohol, and some Italian wines can reach as high as 16%.

Still wines are produced all over the world and can be made in a *dry* and *off-dry* style. This refers to the amount of residual sugar present in the wine. If all the grape sugars have been converted into alcohol, then a wine is considered dry. If the sugars aren't fully converted, or the fermentation is stopped before this happens, the wine is considered off dry. These wines have a distinct impression of sweetness but aren't truly sweet wines.

Still wines come in three colours: red, white, and rosé. Certain grapes are usually associated with certain wine colours but there are exceptions. White wine grapes like Riesling can be made only into white wines, whereas red wine grapes like Pinot Noir can be made into red, rosé, and even white wines like champagne.

Red Wine

Made from dark-skinned grapes, red wine gets its colour from an extended maceration of the must. Typically, maceration can last anywhere from six to 12 days, depending on the desired colour (longer maceration usually results in deeper, darker wines).

> *Punching Down the Cap*
> A fermenting vat of red wine quickly develops a thick layer of skins, pulp,
> and seeds. The juice below will develop little colour unless this layer is
> mixed or pushed down into it. This can be done manually or with a
> machine and is called *remontage* or *foulage*.

In addition to colour, *tannins* are also drawn out of the skins during
maceration. Because tannins are a natural preservative and help wines age,
winemakers try to extract the maximum amount of tannins from the
grape skins to make certain red wines (Cabernet Sauvignon, for example).

Red wines ferment at higher temperatures than white wines and
winemakers may have to use temperature-controlled tanks to raise and
maintain must temperature throughout the process.

Red wines usually receive some ageing in barrels. These can vary in
size from the huge Italian *botte* to the small French *barrique*. The type of
barrel, the wood it is made from, and the length of time the wine stays in
the barrel all affect the wine.

Examples of red wine grapes are Cabernet Sauvignon, Pinot Noir,
Sangiovese, Merlot, and Zinfandel.

White Wine

Made from light-skinned grapes, white wine has to be treated more
carefully than red wine. The grapes are pressed on arrival at the winery to
avoid the risk of oxidation and darkening. A few hours of contact with
the skins at cool temperatures is sometimes allowed to impart more
flavour and fruit character. Since there is essentially no maceration time,
white wine has far fewer tannins than red wine.

White wines ferment at cooler temperatures than red wines.
Temperature-controlled tanks maintain the low temperature throughout
the process to concentrate fruit flavours and to capture freshness in the
wine. This is especially necessary in warm countries such as Chile and
Australia.

Barrel ageing adds an extra dimension to the wine. Too much oak,
however, often masks bad winemaking or poor quality fruit.

Examples of white wine grapes are Chardonnay, Riesling, Sauvignon
Blanc, Sémillon, and Viognier.

> *Softening up Wines*
> Another type of fermentation (malolactic fermentation) occurs
> in most red wines and may be encouraged in some white wines like
> Chardonnay. This softens the harsher (malic) acids in the wine and
> changes them into lactic acids.

Rosé Wine

This may be the most misunderstood style of still wine. Many people
associate rosés with the sweet blush White Zins of California. However,
rosés can also be refreshingly dry wines from the south of France and
Spain.

Rosé wine is made from some of the same grape varieties used to make red wine. There are three ways to make it:

- Macerating red grape must for a few days and fermenting the pale-coloured juice. This is the traditional method;
- Fermenting the juice of quickly pressed red wine grapes, the same way white wine is made. Technically this wine is called a *vin gris*; or
- Fermenting siphoned-off juice from red wine production. This was how White Zin was discovered.

Rosé should never be a blend of white and red grapes (in fact, it is illegal to do so in parts of Europe), but some wineries do it anyway. Rosés are low in tannins (about the same as white wine) and should be consumed right away – they lose freshness over time.

Examples of rosé wine grapes are Grenache, Zinfandel, and Cabernet Franc. But most red wine grapes can be made into rosé.

SPARKLING WINE

While still wine is the wine most people drink on a day-to-day basis, sparkling wine is the wine we suspect they would like to drink more often. And why not? It is fun to drink and is usually associated with happy events – weddings and ship launchings. Sparkling wine, unfortunately, is rarely considered as a wine to be served with a meal.

Sparkling wines are produced all over the world and can be made in various styles and sweetness levels. Most sparkling wine has between 8% and 12% alcohol by volume. The most prestigious, and the most famous, sparkling wine is champagne.

What is the difference between sparkling wine and still wine? In a word, bubbles. Carbon dioxide is a byproduct of fermentation, and instead of letting the carbon dioxide escape into the air, as it does with still wine, the gas is made to dissolve or be absorbed into the wine. This is done in one of three ways:

- A second fermentation in the bottle;
- A second fermentation in the tank; or
- Carbonation.

A second fermentation happens when more yeast and sugar are added to already fermented wine. For carbonation you hook up a CO_2 tank to some wine and hey presto, sparkling wine.

In the Bottle

The first method is usually associated with champagne. Since only sparkling wine made in France in the region of Champagne can legally be called *champagne*, all other sparkling wines made this way must use the term *méthode traditionelle* or "traditional method" on the label. So if you see "champagne" on the label, you know you're drinking the "real thing."

Red Grapes Make White Wine?
Pinot Noir and Pinot Meunier are both dark-skinned grapes yet they are used to make a white wine – champagne. How so? In making the base wine, the grapes are almost immediately pressed, and the skins are not allowed to macerate at all.

All sparkling wines, including champagne, begin as still wine. By law, champagne can be made using only Chardonnay, Pinot Noir, Pinot Meunier, or a combination of these grapes. Other sparkling wines made using the *méthode traditionelle* may use different grapes and many of these are unique to the region or country. The Prosecco grape, for example, is used to make very enjoyable sparkling wine in the Veneto region of Italy.

Depending on the house style of the producer, different still wines are first blended together. This is called *assemblage*. A measured amount of yeast and sugar is added to the blend to start a second fermentation, and the wine is bottled. The bottle used for champagne is much heavier than a usual wine bottle as a considerable amount of pressure builds up during the second fermentation. This is also the bottle you will see when you buy the wine, but the cap used at this point is temporary and looks like a beer cap.

The wine is stored (in vast underground chalk tunnels in Champagne) until the second fermentation has stopped and the wine has properly interacted with the *lees* (spent yeast cells) to acquire the characteristic fine bubbles and toasty aromas. This can take as little as a few months for sparkling wine or as long as three years for vintage champagne (non-vintage champagne is required by law to rest for 15 months). The longer, the better.

Big Pressure
The pressure in a bottle of champagne, which is as much as 90 pounds per square inch (six atmospheres), is enough to fill a bus or lorry tyre.

Lees are unsightly – sort of a cloudy blob – and have to be removed without losing all the fizz that has built up. Through a complicated and slow process of manipulation called *remuage*, the *riddler*, as he is called in Champagne, works with the bottle until the sediment collects at the neck. The neck is then dipped in a cooling liquid to freeze the sediment and the cap is removed. The pressure that has built up in the bottle forces out the frozen blob, leaving the wine clean and bubbly. Here's a word to impress your friends: this process is called *dégorgement* (disgorgement).

A little wine is added to the bottle to replace what may have been lost. The winemaker may add sweetened wine (*dosage*) if a sweeter style of sparkling wine is desired; otherwise, champagne is dry. Finally, the bottle is corked – that big fat mushroom-cap-shaped cork – and fitted with a protective cage. The pressure in the bottle is far too great for standard corks, and sparkling wine producers don't want any of that sparkle to be lost until you open your bottle to toast your next celebration.

As a rule, sparkling wine – even champagne – should be consumed soon after purchase. The winery has stored it for you and determined when it is ready to drink. The very best vintage champagne can age and should be treated the same way you would a very good white wine – with respect.

Two examples of non-champagne sparkling wines produced this way include Cava (in Spain) and Crémant (in France).

In the Tank

Lower priced sparklers are made by allowing the second fermentation to occur in a large sealed tank instead of the bottle. This is called the *Charmat*, *bulk*, or *tank* method. It is unlikely that you will see this listed on the label; however, if it doesn't say "champagne" or "méthode traditionelle," assume this method was used.

Essentially the whole process occurs in "bulk," in a tank instead of the bottle. The yeast and sugar necessary to start the second fermentation are added to the blended wine in the tank. The fermentation builds up carbon dioxide, and again this gas is absorbed into the wine. Once the fermentation is complete, the wine is filtered and bottled while still under pressure. The whole process can take only months instead of years; therefore, wineries can adapt to market conditions much faster than the big champagne houses.

The bubbles produced using this method are generally larger and not as long living as those of champagne. If you don't mind slightly larger bubbles or are planning to make cocktails with it, there are some excellent wines out there for you to try. Italian Asti and German Sekt (for example, Henkel Trocken), are two lower-priced alternatives that still offer up the fun of more expensive sparklers.

All Gassed Up

The cheapest way to make sparkling wine is by using carbonation. This is akin to making soda water and the result is sometimes no better than cream soda. The bubbles are very large and often disappear before you have your first sip. The price difference between carbonated and tank method sparklers is very little, so spend the extra money.

The Secret of Those Big Bottles
A slight variation of the méthode traditionelle, called the transfer method, is used to speed up the process and make good sparkling wine at a lower price. To avoid the slow remuage process, wineries empty the contents of the bottles into a pressurized tank, then filter out the lees. The wine is then re-bottled into new, less expensive bottles and sold. There may be fewer bubbles or less complex aromas using this method, but the result is still an excellent sparkling wine. FYI, this is also how they produce those huge bottles of champagne they use to celebrate the end of a Formula One race.

FORTIFIED WINE

We are often asked if fortified wine is in fact wine at all. The answer is yes. The only major difference between still and fortified wines is that alcohol has been added to the latter at some stage in the winemaking process.

There are two main types of fortified wines:

- Wines in which alcohol is used to stop fermentation *before* it is complete; and
- Wines in which alcohol is added *after* fermentation is finished.

Wines in the first category (port, for example) are generally sweeter than those in the second category (sherry, for example). All fortified wines are stronger than still wines, having an alcohol content somewhere in the range of 18% to 20%.

Port

 Many countries use the term *port*, but *porto*, like champagne, is the proprietary name given to fortified wine produced in the Douro region of northern Portugal. However, for simplicity, we will use the term port for wines fortified *before* fermentation is complete.

When you drink a glass of port you will notice three things. First, unless it is white port, it has a relatively deep, dark red colour. Next, its alcohol content is somewhat high. Third, it's sweet. These three characteristics result from the unique way port is made.

The speedy extraction of colour and tannins is important to port. Remember, tannins are a preservative, and port usually needs to be stored for years before it is drinkable. Winemakers must work quickly because they need to fortify the wine before fermentation is complete.

After two to three days of maceration, the wine reaches the right sweetness level (about 6% to 8% alcohol) and is considered ready for fortification. The wine is added to a neutral spirit (77% alcohol called *aguardente*) to kill off the yeasts and stop the fermentation. The resulting wine contains about 20% alcohol with some residual sugar. The port is then placed in a wooden barrel called a *pipe* for ageing.

Depending on the vineyard, the quality of the grapes, and the needs of the market, different types of port (see page 114) can be made from this wine.

These Feet Were Made for Treading

The traditional method to extract colour quickly was to tread the grapes, usually to music. The foot is perfectly designed to apply the right amount of pressure without bruising the grapes or breaking the pips. In about one day, a team of highly skilled treaders will extract the right amount of colour and tannins from the grapes. Don't worry, everyone's feet are checked for cleanliness before they are allowed into the vat.

Madeira

Just off the coast of Portugal is an island called Madeira. Here they make a fortified wine called – you guessed it – madeira. What makes this wine unique is that it is literally cooked (sometimes for years), either under the sun, in *estufas* (tanks warmed by heaters), or in steam lodges (rooms or buildings heated by steam). This caramelizes the sugars in the wine and promotes oxidation – usually undesirable in wine, but good for madeira. The best madeira is given 20 or more years of barrel ageing.

For the sweeter styles of madeira (Bual and Malmsey), alcohol is added to stop fermentation (like port). For the drier versions (Sercial), the alcohol is added after fermentation is complete (like sherry). Verdelho is a medium-sweet style of madeira.

Cooked Wine

Madeira was an important trading stop for ships on their way to Africa and the New World. Traders fortified the local wine so that it would not go bad on the long voyages. It was then discovered that the wine actually improved with exposure to the sweltering heat as the ships crossed the equator and so madeira was born.

Sherry

Sherry is the generic name given to wines fortified *after* fermentation is complete. Real sherry – one of the world's greatest wine secrets – since the 1990s must come from the south of Spain and takes its name from the town of Jerez.

Much to the surprise of most people, sherry is usually dry, not sweet. Because the wine is allowed to fully ferment before the fortifying spirit is added, there is no residual sugar in it. There are some sweet sherries that have been sweetened (and probably coloured) artificially or with sweet grape juice, but sherry is generally dry and consumed as an apéritif.

SOLERA SYSTEM

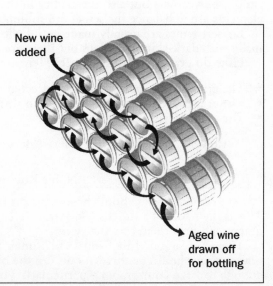

New wine added

The solera is a progressive ageing process whereby the oldest wine is drawn off from the last barrel, then replaced by wine from the previous barrel and so on.

Aged wine drawn off for bottling

Unlike port, sherry is made from light-skinned wine grapes. And like a white wine, the juice is pressed off the skins and allowed to ferment, then it is fortified.

Wine made from the best grapes, usually Palomino, grown in the best soil, will be made in the *fino* style and fortified up to about 15.5% alcohol. This is the ideal level for *flor* to develop. Flor is a yeast that forms on the surface of the wine and feeds off the alcohol in the wine and the oxygen in the barrel. In turn, it reduces the overall acidity of the wine and gives it a dry, clean, tangy taste.

If the wine isn't going to be a fino, then it will be made into an *oloroso* and fortified to about 18%. This prevents the flor from developing. Oloroso is also dry, but with raisiny, nutty, burnt toffee aromas and flavours.

Both fino and oloroso are then aged in a *solera* – a series of barrels – until ready for sale.

Flor and the solera are unique to true sherry and are rarely reproduced elsewhere. Sherry-style wines made in Cyprus or South Africa are usually sweeter and can't really be compared to the original.

DESSERT WINE

These wines are much sweeter than regular still wines. Not regular off-dry sweet, like a White Zin or an off-dry Riesling. We're talking super-sweet: from 20 grams to as much as 500 grams per litre of unfermented sugar. Sometimes called sweeties, stickies, or even pudding wines, dessert wines are among some of the greatest wines in the world, yet they are a relatively obscure category for most people. Stick with us and we will help change this perspective.

To make luscious, rich sweet wines you need grapes that are so ripe that the yeasts cannot ferment all the sugar before they are zapped by high alcohol levels. When the yeasts stop working lots of sugar will be left in the fermented wine. The key to greatness and longevity, however, isn't just sweetness but also the acidity in the grapes. When these two elements are in balance the wines are sublime.

Dessert wines are usually made with light-skinned grapes. A few are made with dark-skinned grapes but these are the exception.

How do grapes get super-sweet? Here are three ways:

- The grapes are encouraged to be affected by "noble rot," a fungus;
- The grapes are air dried or allowed to shrivel up (i.e., "raisining"); or
- The grapes freeze on the vine.

Whatever the method, the result is "dessert in a glass."

Noble Rot

No, we're not talking about cheap wine drunk at Buckingham Palace. This is the name of a fungus (*Botrytis cinerea*) that is allowed to attack grapes and help them become sweet.

There are "good" fungi and "bad" fungi. If the "bad" type affects the grapes, they should be thrown out. On the other hand if you are lucky enough to have your grapes – particularly your white wine grapes –

affected by the benevolent form then you are indeed blessed. "Noble rot"
– or *pourriture noble*, if you prefer – consumes the water stored inside the
grape, thereby concentrating the sugars. The resulting sugar levels are
many times higher than those in regular grapes, so that a lot more
residual sugar remains in the wine after fermentation has finished.

Grapes can also become sweeter if they hang on the vine long after the
harvest is over. Wines made from these grapes are less sweet than the
noble rot versions and are usually called *late harvest* wines.

The most famous, and usually the most expensive, version of sweet wine
made by grapes affected by noble rot is Sauternes from Bordeaux. The one
that has been made the longest, though, is Tokaji Aszú of Hungary,
predating Sauternes by some 200 years. Botrytized wines are also made in
other countries including Australia, Chile, the United States, and Canada.

Dried Grapes

A number of different wines fall under this category – even to some extent
late harvest wines – but essentially these are wines made from dried
grapes. Italian winemakers are famous for making *passito* wines by picking
grapes and drying the bunches for many months. This shrivels up or
"raisins" the grapes and concentrates the sugars. Vin Santo from Tuscany
and Recioto from Veneto are perhaps the most famous passito wines.

Many other traditional air-dried wines are now fortified, but in France
true *vin de paille*, as it is called, is still made in the Jura region. In Austria,
some winemakers still dry their grapes on straw mats. Here, the wine is
called *Strohwein*.

Icewine

Finally, there is icewine. While some winemakers in California are using
cryo-extraction (post-harvest freezing in a freezer), *real* icewine is made
by allowing the grapes to freeze naturally on the vine. This is possible in
only a few places, Canada, the northern United States, Germany (where it
is called Eiswein), Austria, and parts of Eastern Europe.

The grapes are left on the vine until December or January, when the
temperature drops to 18°F (–8°C) or colder for a few days. It is important
to note that the grapes are picked *and* pressed at this temperature; if the
must is allowed to warm above this temperature, by law the wine is no
longer icewine and becomes essentially very expensive late harvest wine.

When the frozen grapes are pressed, only the sticky sweet juice comes
out. The water remains frozen with the rest of the grape, leaving the must
very concentrated. As you can imagine, it takes a long time to extract
sufficient juice to make icewine. This, to a certain extent, justifies the high
prices these wines command. The resulting wine is pure nectar and, at
times, worth every penny.

Icewine is usually made with light-skinned grapes, mainly Riesling
and Vidal. A number of wineries in Canada are also experimenting with
dark-skinned grapes but the supply is very limited. If you aren't hung up
on whether the grapes have been naturally frozen or not, look for some
value-priced versions (by law now they can't be called icewine) made
with commercially frozen grapes – Vin de Glacière as one Californian
winemaker calls it.

AROMATIZED WINE

Vermouth is probably the best known example of "aromatized" or flavoured wine. There are different, and sometimes ancient, recipes for making aromatized wines, but whatever the formula, it usually involves macerating spices, fruits, or herbs in a base wine and sometimes adding sugar for sweetness and caramel for colour. Some wines – especially French vermouth – are aged in barrels, but this isn't necessary.

In general, Italian vermouth is red and sweet, while French versions are gold and drier. While vermouth is fortified, Greek *retsina* is an example of an unfortified flavoured wine. Wine coolers also fall into this category.

IS WINE GOOD FOR YOU?

Are any of these wines – still, sparkling, or especially, dessert – good for you? Only your doctor can really answer that question. Nonetheless you may have heard of the French Paradox – people in France with high-fat diets drinking red wine and enjoying some of the lowest rates of heart disease in the world. When this connection was publicized in the early 1990s, red wine consumption rose. It's been on the increase ever since. It turns out there's something in red wine – and in red grape juice – with medicinal properties.

Throughout history, wine was thought to have healing benefits. Until recently, there hadn't been much research to support this. Increasingly, medical research is finding links between the moderate consumption of wine and a range of health benefits. Guidelines suggest "moderate" means one to two standard glasses per day. However, guidelines don't apply to individuals equally. How you metabolize alcohol and how it affects your health will depend on your age, gender, body type, state of health, any medications you are taking, and whether you are drinking on a full or empty stomach. Your predisposition will determine what amount of wine can be consumed without damage to your overall health.

The Good

Wine, in particular red wine, is full of antioxidant compounds or phenolics. The most famous of these is resveratrol. It helps improve the balance between the "good" HDL cholesterol and the "bad" LDL cholesterol, providing a protective effect against cardiovascular disease. As a bonus for those who prefer cool climate wines, higher concentrations of resveratrol are found in red wines from regions like Burgundy and New Zealand.

There's a connection between moderate wine consumption and improved digestion. The polyphenols in wine seem to have antibacterial properties, wiping out certain bacteria connected to food poisoning and inhibiting a strain that causes ulcers.

Other beneficial effects associated with the consumption of red wine include reduced hypertension, improved bone density, and a strengthened immune system. And, of course, there's the relaxation factor. Results of a recent Danish study also suggest wine drinking is associated with improved social, intellectual, and personality functions.

The Bad

But along with the good comes the bad. Wine contains negative components that can damage your health and well-being. Alcohol, for example, is a toxin. Beyond moderate levels, it has a damaging effect on the body.

Fortunately, a hangover is entirely preventable. Besides drinking less when you drink, have a glass of water before, during, or after each glass of wine. And never drink on an empty stomach. Food slows down the rate of alcohol absorption into the bloodstream and makes it easier on your system.

Alcohol consumption, which has long had an association with fetal alcohol syndrome, is not advised for women who are pregnant or for nursing mothers.

Finally, be aware that the alcohol in wine makes it full of calories – ranging from 90 calories for a light-bodied red or white still wine to 135 calories for a glass of port or sweet wine.

Wine and Allergies

Other than a hangover, does drinking red wine ever give you a headache? Or perhaps you avoid white wine because it makes you break out in a rash? If so, you may have sensitivities to certain components in wines which cause an allergic reaction.

An allergic reaction to red wine is likely due to the naturally occurring amines known as histamines (which dilate the blood vessels in the brain) or tyramines (which constrict them) in the wine. White wines are generally lower in amines than red wines, though you can experiment with red wines to find ones with lower levels of this allergen.

Allergic reactions to white wine are more likely caused by the presence of sulphites in the wine. Sulphur dioxide is used as a preservative in wines – white wines especially – to inhibit oxidation and the growth of moulds and bacteria. Your reaction may be due to either high sensitivity or excessive use of sulphur in the winemaking process. To find out whether you have to rule out white wines altogether, try organic white wines. If you still have a reaction, you're the sensitive type and it may just be best to avoid them.

The Ugly

You may think you're clueless about wine, but you shouldn't be about drinking and driving. It goes without saying that *any* amount of alcohol, whether beer, spirits, or wine, is unsafe if you are driving.

It's worth knowing that 5 oz (140 ml) of wine is equivalent to 1½ oz (45 ml) of spirits and 12 oz (340 ml) of beer. This formula is based on an average 12% alcohol wine. Adjust accordingly if you're drinking an 8% German Riesling or a 15% Zinfandel.

When consumed in moderation as part of a healthy diet and lifestyle, wine can be beneficial to your health. On the other hand, only your doctor can tell you whether moderate alcohol consumption will bring benefits or pose risks. To quote the Chinese proverb, "Wine should be taken in small doses, knowledge in large ones."

WHERE IN THE WORLD DOES WINE COME FROM?

AROUND THE WINE WORLD IN ABOUT 50 PAGES

Until such time as all wine shops and restaurant wine lists are organized by grape variety or style, you'll need to know something about the places where grapes are grown and wine is made. About 60 countries produce a meaningful amount of wine, and at most half of those have wines represented in a typical large supermarket. We'll focus on those that you are most likely to encounter.

Some of these wines will be *Old World* and some *New World*. In winespeak, these terms are used to emphasize differences in winemaking techniques or styles rather than geographic borders.

When we use Old World we are referring to Europe and the Mediterranean basin, covering about three-quarters of the world's vineyards and wine production. The New World refers to the Americas, South Africa, Australia, and New Zealand.

The Old World, in a wine context, is about tradition and place. Growers and winemakers have had about 4,000 years to identify which grape varieties are the best to grow and make into good wine. The Old World also captures the culture of wine drinking. Wine is considered an everyday drink rather than something kept for special occasions. It's less often drunk as a cocktail and more to accompany food.

In contrast, the New World is more about science than tradition. Grape growing and winemaking are less established (only about 400 years) and the lack of tradition and rules has allowed the ready adoption of new technologies. With a few exceptions, wine is the alcoholic beverage of choice for a small percentage of the population (for example, less than one-third of Americans drink wine regularly), and the culture of food and wine is only now catching up to the rest of the world.

These differences are less clear-cut than they used to be. Old World producers are embracing technological innovations and New World producers see the value – if only a marketing one for some – of *terroir*.

DECIPHERING ALL THOSE INITIALS

Most Old World wine-producing countries have some way of classifying their wines. A number of New World countries – Canada, the United States, Australia, New Zealand, and South Africa, for example – are also getting around to doing this. Essentially what these classification systems do is guarantee that the wine you are buying comes from the region (the rules define or *delimit* the region), possesses the character of the region (e.g., Bordeaux wine smells and tastes like Bordeaux wine), and has been made in accordance with the rules and regulations of the region.

Each classification system has a hierarchical series of levels or categories. The chart below indicates the names and initials used by the major Old World wine-producing countries:

Classification	France	Italy	Germany	Spain	Portugal
Table wine	Vin de table	Vino da tavola	Tafelwein	Vino de mesa	Vinho de mesa
Regional wine	Vin de pays	IGT Indicazione Geografica Tipica	Landwein	Vino de la tierra	Vinho regional
Quality wine	AC Appellation d'Origine Contrôlée	DOC Denominazione di Origine Controllata	QbA Qualitätswein bestimmter Anbaugebeite	DO Denominación de Origen	DOC Denominação de Origem Controlada
Wine with distinction		DOCG Denominazione di Origine Controllata e Garantita	QmP Qualitätswein mit Prädikat	DOCa Denominación de Origen Calificada	

Table wine is the lowest level of classification and there is no reference to place of origin, vintage, or even the grapes on the label.

Regional wines or "country wines" indicate the place of origin on the label. Responding to international demand, producers usually list the grape varieties as well.

Table and regional wines represent a large proportion of each country's wine production – sometimes more than half. Prices for these wines are good and they usually deliver fair value for money. Some of Italy's IGT or *vino da tavola* wines are much superior to other wines in the same category because the producers have chosen not to be included in the higher Quality category, or because, according to officials, they do not conform to local regulations and have been banned from being included in the higher category.

Quality wines are usually the highest-level classification for wines. They conform to the strictest regulations and offer the best guarantee of authenticity.

Wines with distinction are unique or historically defined wines (e.g., Barolo). Occasionally the regulations are higher, and tighter, than those for Quality wines, but the distinction is mainly for political or historical reasons.

Each country or region has its own version of these classifications. It is important to remember that these classifications *do not*, despite their intentions or names, provide a guarantee of quality.

In the New World, the classification systems are usually one-tiered. A wine is either in the classification or it isn't. But in all cases the guarantee is essentially the same: the wine/grapes come from the region, have been made in accordance with the rules and regulations of the region, and to some extent possess the character of the region (though that is less of an issue in the New World). In the United States AVAs (American Viticultural Areas) are used to delimit wine regions; in Canada it is VQA (Vintner's Quality Alliance); in Australia they use GIS (Geographic Indications System); and in South Africa it's WO (Wines of Origin).

Judging Wine by Its Label

Wine labels differ greatly from country to country, even region to region. New World wineries tend to feature the grape name prominently: "Chardonnay" or "Cabernet Sauvignon." Some Old World regions – Germany, Alsace, Friuli in Italy, and most Eastern European countries – also use the grape name approach. They are the exception, though, not the rule.

Old World wineries tend to use regional or *terroir*-based labelling styles: for example, Chianti Classico (Italy) or Ribera del Duero (Spain). The strict laws of these regions dictate which grapes can be grown there, so it's assumed you know which grape or grapes were used in making the wine.

The third type of wine label omits both varietal and geographic information. Some examples are Gentil (a blend of white grapes from Alsace), Ornellaia (Merlot from Italy), and Noble One (Sémillon-based dessert wine from Australia). In many cases, these are higher end wines made by producers who want to use grape varieties not permitted by local authorities.

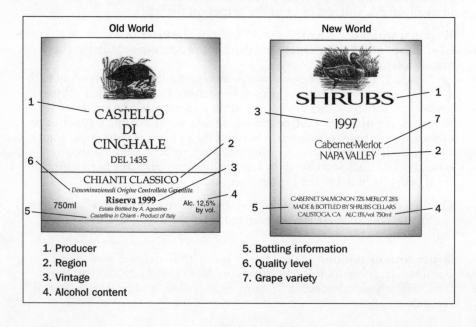

1. Producer
2. Region
3. Vintage
4. Alcohol content
5. Bottling information
6. Quality level
7. Grape variety

They say you can't judge a book by its cover, but you usually can tell a lot about the wine from the label. Here are the key things you'll find on most wine labels and what they mean:

- **Producer's name** – If you are familiar with the producer, this can be an indication of the wine's style and quality.
- **Vintage** – The wine's age tells you whether to expect something youthful or mature. If you know the vintage was good or bad in the region, this may be an indicator of the wine's quality.
- **Region** – This is where the wine comes from. The more precise the region (e.g., a single vineyard), the higher the quality and likewise the price.
- **Grape variety** – You will always see this stated on a New World wine, and also on some Old World wines.
- **Alcohol content** – Stated as a percentage of volume. Most still wines will be around 12%. Fortified wines will be higher.
- **Bottling information** – This indicates where the wine was bottled (the winery or a large commercial factory). You might see *mise en bouteille au château, domaine,* or *à la propriété* on French labels, and *imbottigliato* on Italian labels.
- **Classification** – For those countries with a classification system for wines, these usually appear as an acronym on the label. For example, VQA, AC, AVA, DOCa, QmP, or DOC.

Spin the bottle around to see what else the winery has to say about its wine. You may find a little map of the winery's location, some information on the grape varieties in the wine, how dry or sweet the wine is, how much oakiness to expect, foods to pair with it, or serving temperatures. Understand that what you read on the back label is there to help sell you on that wine over another. Some of the more famous wines provide no back label information, presuming the wine speaks for itself.

FRANCE

France is indisputably the "mother ship" of fine wine production. It produces over 20% of the world's wine and is home to some of the world's greatest brands and regions. France also sets the standard for six of the Top Seven wine grapes: Cabernet Sauvignon, Chardonnay, Syrah, Pinot Noir, Merlot, and Sauvignon Blanc. Perhaps only in Italy is the link between wine and culture as strong as it is in France.

Wine Classification

France was the first country to establish regulations for wine production. Among other things, these regulations delimit areas of production, approve method of production, and control yields, alcohol levels, and grape varieties.

Vintages

Vintages matter in France because its weather is quite variable, especially in certain parts of the country. An exceptional vintage can produce exceptional wines that will last decades, while in a so-so year the wines may be okay but not ageworthy. Prices can skyrocket in outstanding vintages, like 2000.

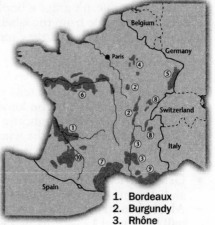

Producers

Although price may be an indicator of quality, the most reliable way to guarantee quality is to know the producer. Even in bad vintages, good producers can make good wine. In some regions wine brokers – *négociants* – buy grapes, juice, or even finished wine and bottle it under their own label.

1. Bordeaux
2. Burgundy
3. Rhône
4. Champagne
5. Alsace
6. Loire
7. Languedoc-Rousillon
8. Jura-Savoie
9. Provence
10. The Southwest

Regional Identification on the Label

There are a dozen major wine regions in France and the focus of French wine is on the area of production – the *appellation* – and not on the grape variety. This is important because most bottles of French wine show only the appellation on the label, not the type of grape used. Only AC wines from Alsace and some smaller regional wines (for example, Vin de Pays d'Oc) include the grape variety on the label.

Due to soil, site, and climate (the *terroir*), some appellations will produce better wines than others, and the more specific the information on the bottle, the easier it is to work this out. When a village or vineyard name appears on the label, the wine will be much better than if, for example, it says Burgundy, or even just France.

As a place to start, you'll need to know four regions: Bordeaux, Burgundy, Rhône, and Champagne. These are the most influential internationally.

> *Buying Tip*
> In good vintages, pick a lesser producer. In lesser vintages, pick a good producer.

Bordeaux

Located in the southwest, Bordeaux is France's largest quality wine-producing region, producing about a quarter of the country's total output of AC wine. All French wines benefit from the international reputation of Bordeaux. Some of the most expensive and sought-after red wines in the world are produced here, as well as one of the world's greatest sweet wines – Sauternes. However, despite the region's exalted reputation, the majority of wine produced in Bordeaux is just basic AC Bordeaux.

Main AC Regions
Bordeaux
Burgundy
Rhône
Champagne
Alsace
Loire
Languedoc-Roussillon
Provence

Location, location, appellation!

In Bordeaux, location matters. Each of its 10 districts are characterized by soil composition, climate, the grapes that are grown there, vineyard owners, and traditions. The price and quality of the wine vary accordingly. Simply being on the wrong side of a dividing line can mean the difference between selling a wine for £100 or for £10.

The wine districts of Bordeaux hug the banks of three rivers: the Gironde, Garonne, and Dordogne. Vineyards to the north of the Gironde are said to be on the *Right Bank* and those on the south side are on the *Left Bank*. In the middle, between the Garonne and Dordogne rivers, is *Entre-Deux-Mers* – literally "between two seas." The Bordelais always think big!

While each district produces different wines, some generalizations can be made about the wines from each of these larger areas:

> **Key Districts**
> **Left Bank:**
> Haut-Médoc,
> Graves, and
> Sauternes;
> **Right Bank:**
> St-Émilion
> **Entre-Deux-Mers**

- *Left Bank* red wines are more austere, ageworthy, and tannic. The dry whites are big, powerful wines, while the sweet wines are decadent nectar.
- *Right Bank* red wines are richer, fruitier, and more approachable. They are the best introductory red wines for Bordeaux. They are also safer choices on restaurant wine lists, especially if they are at least five years old. The Right Bank is not known for its white wines.
- *Entre-Deux-Mers* is better known for its crisp, fresh, dry white wines but it also produces oceans of straightforward easy drinking reds. These too are safe bets on a wine list.

The districts are further subdivided into *communes* (meaning "villages") – the highest level of appellation possible. It is at this level that the biggest distinctions in terms of price are made. The top wines are made in the top communes.

> **Top Communes**
> **Left Bank:**
> Pauillac, Margaux,
> St-Julien, and
> Pessac-Léognan;
> **Right Bank:**
> Pomerol

Bordeaux wines are blends

Bordeaux wines aren't made from one grape. They're actually blends of grapes – reds with reds and whites with whites.

Red Bordeaux is generally a blend of Cabernet Sauvignon and Merlot with quantities of Cabernet Franc, Malbec, and Petit Verdot added depending on harvest conditions and the style of the winery. Cabernet Sauvignon is the dominant grape in the Left Bank, Merlot in the Right Bank, but Merlot is most planted overall.

With all the fuss about Bordeaux's red wines, it is easy to overlook its excellent white wines. Sauvignon Blanc is used on its own to make inexpensive, crisp, dry, and citrus-flavoured whites or is blended with Sémillon and Muscadelle to create more lush and smooth wines. The best dry white wines come from Pessac-Léognan.

> **Key Bordeaux Grapes**
> **Red:**
> Cabernet
> Sauvignon,
> Merlot, and
> Cabernet Franc;
> **White:**
> Sauvignon Blanc
> and Sémillon

Bordeaux also makes decadently sweet wines: the most famous being Sauternes. These are made primarily with Sémillon but with some Sauvignon Blanc and Muscadelle blended in for acidity, aromatics, and structure. Lesser known, good value sweet wines are also produced in Cadillac and Loupiac.

Bordeaux wines are classified

For easy identification, Bordeaux wines are usually bottled in high-shoulder bottles. Its classification system for AC wines has three levels:

- *Regional* (e.g., Bordeaux or Bordeaux Supérieur). These are inexpensive wines with a consistent style, but don't expect quality. The larger producers may label their wines with a proprietary name (e.g., Mouton Cadet).
- *District* (e.g., Entre-Deux-Mers). This is a step up in quality. The name of the district will appear on the label.
- *Commune* (e.g., Margaux). This is the highest level appellation within a district.

But now it gets a bit more complicated. The Médoc and Sauternes-Barsac districts (on the Left Bank) are further classified according to properties, known as Châteaux. This classification ranked all properties according to the price of their wines in 1855. Of the five ranks, or *cru classés* (classed growths), the best and most famous are the *premiers crus* (first growths) followed by *deuxièmes crus* (second growths), and so on.

> *Official First Growths:*
> *The 1855 Classification*
> Château Margaux
> Château Latour
> Château Lafite-Rothschild
> Château Haut-Brion
> Château Mouton-Rothschild
> (was added in 1973)

Not to be outdone, the Right Bank came up with a separate classification system (created in 1955), as did Graves on the Left Bank four years later. To further complicate things, not every property is classified under one of these systems: there are now a few hundred *cru bourgeois* producing excellent wines that represent, at times, better value than some of the crus classés. Perhaps Bordeaux wines should be *certified*, not classified!

Is Bordeaux affordable?

With all this talk of Châteaux and premiers crus, Bordeaux does sound expensive. Well, it doesn't have to be. Top crus like Pétrus (from Pomerol in the Right Bank) will cost you hundreds of pounds but a humble AC Bordeaux wine can set you back around £5.

Between the two there are thousands of different Bordeaux wines, at all price points.

Here are a few buying tips:

- District wines, for example Entre-Deux-Mers, are usually good value, but drink them right away. André Lurton is a good producer.
- Cru bourgeois are often well made, good quality wines, but not nearly as expensive as the crus classés.

> **Châteaux**
> In Bordeaux, the name of the Château that makes the wine can be important. Generally, wines from these producers represent the best quality and command the highest prices. Châteaux aren't always grand castles, though some are, but are more likely to be simple estates.

- Look for the "second label" of a major Château. Carruades de Lafite, for example, is the second label of Lafite-Rothschild and may include wine that would normally go into their top cru. Mouton Cadet, however, is no longer the second label for Mouton-Rothschild.
- Buy from lesser-known districts or communes. The commune Moulis, for example, is right next door to the famous Margaux and some of its producers are also capable of making full-bodied, ageworthy wines.

> **Bargain Districts**
> Côtes de Bourg
> Côtes de Blaye
> Fronsac
> Entre-Deux-Mers

Burgundy

Burgundy lies southeast of Paris and forms a long strip, much of it an escarpment, some 115 miles (185 kilometres) long. It shares Bordeaux's distinction of producing some of the most expensive and sought-after red and white wines in the world.

Burgundy's climate is often cool and damp with the occasional hot summer. There can be even greater variations in vintages than in Bordeaux. Soil composition, exposure to the sun, and the altitude and steepness of the slope (the better vineyards are situated around the mid-point of the slopes and face due east) also contribute greatly to the diversity of the wines from this region.

> **Key Grapes**
> **Red:**
> **Pinot Noir and Gamay;**
> **White:**
> **Chardonnay**

Hooked on classics

Unlike wines from Bordeaux, Burgundian wines are made from essentially two grapes – Pinot Noir and Chardonnay – and there is no blending. When conditions are perfect, the wines produced from these grapes may be the most sublime anywhere. When the conditions are poor, it's a good time to look elsewhere. Vintages really do matter in Burgundy.

Red Burgundy is Pinot Noir. At its prime, this wine is sensuous and silky with exotic raspberry, plum, and earthy truffle aromas, but in poor vintages it can be thin and tart. Winemaking is still traditional (no new oak) so the wines are subtler than New World Pinot Noirs. Basic Burgundy (Bourgogne Rouge) will be less complex but still nice and fruity. Unless you're sure of the vintage, Pinot Noir from Burgundy is a risky choice on a wine list.

White Burgundy is Chardonnay and, like Pinot Noir, it is at its best in Burgundy. Done well, it has few equals. Burgundian Chardonnay, however, appears to take on multiple personalities based on the area where the grapes are grown:

- In the north, wines from Chablis are austere and crisp with appley aromas.
- Farther south, Chardonnay can be rich and buttery (in Meursault) or creamy and nutty (in Puligny-Montrachet).
- Even farther south, in Mâcon, Chardonnay is medium bodied, fresh, and lively. And the price will be much less. Mâcon-Villages is an excellent starting point for white Burgundy and probably represents a safe choice on a wine list.

Pyramid power

Burgundy wines are usually bottled in slope-shouldered bottles. The classification system here – originally drawn up in 1861 – is a four-step hierarchical system, based on local practices and natural factors such as soil type. It seems simple enough, but when you throw in 10,000 vineyards it gets kind of wacky. Almost 25% of France's AC wines come from Burgundy and over 500 *climats* ("plots") are classed as premier cru.

A pyramid is a good way to visualize it. As you move up the pyramid, quality and price increase while availability decreases:

- *Regional* wines, red or white, can be made from grapes grown anywhere in Burgundy. The simplest are called AC *Bourgogne* (French for Burgundy). Grape names (e.g., Bourgogne Aligoté) and districts (e.g., Mâcon) may be added to the label as long as the wine meets certain requirements.
- *Commune* or *village* appellation wines indicate that the grapes come from a particular wine-producing commune. There are about 40 of these appellations and the name of the commune (e.g., Volnay) appears prominently on the label.

Key Communes
Gevrey-Chambertin
Morey-St-Denis
Chambolle-Musigny
Vougeot
Flagey-Échézeaux
Vosne-Romanée
Nuits-St-Georges
Aloxe-Corton
Puligny-Montrachet
Chassagne-Montrachet

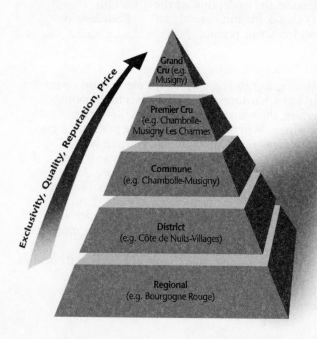

Exclusivity, Quality, Reputation, Price

Grand Cru (e.g. Musigny)

Premier Cru (e.g. Chambolle-Musigny Les Charmes)

Commune (e.g. Chambolle-Musigny)

District (e.g. Côte de Nuits-Villages)

Regional (e.g. Bourgogne Rouge)

- *Premier crus* (1er cru) aren't specifically appellations but are better categorized as a special class of commune. At last count there were over 560 premiers crus. The label shows the commune, in larger letters, followed by the specific vineyard where the grapes were grown, for example, Volnay Les Caillerets.
- *Grand cru* represents the very best vineyard locations and each one has its own appellation. There are 40 grand cru appellations (seven of which are in Chablis) yet they represent only about 2% of total wine production. Only the vineyard name (e.g., Le Montrachet) appears on the label.

Who's who?

Here's where Burgundy gets confusing. More than one winemaker may have access to the same vineyard. In fact, much of the output from the land is sold to larger wineries. As a consumer, it is important to know who these companies are. In Burgundy they are known as *négociants* – individuals or companies who buy grapes, juice, and/or wine and bottle it under their own name. About 80% of Burgundian wine is sold through négociants. Some of the top, or more reputable, négociants include Joseph Drouhin, Bouchard Père et Fils, Louis Jadot, Jaffelin, and Louis Latour.

And where's where?

Burgundy is made up of five diverse districts: Chablis, Côte d'Or, Côte Chalonnaise, Mâconnais, and Beaujolais.

Chablis is the most northerly district and is mainly known for Chardonnay. But these Chardonnays may be different than you are used to – nervy, flinty, with fairly high acidity. They become more likeable as they age.

Côte d'Or is the spiritual centre for Burgundian wine lovers. Here are the vineyards that produce arguably some of the best Pinot Noir and Chardonnay in the world. The area is further broken into two subdistricts with the city of Beaune as roughly the dividing point:

- **Côte de Nuits**, north of Beaune, is known for glorious Pinot Noir. Here you'll find communes such as Nuits-Saint-Georges, Vosne-Romanée, and Gevrey-Chambertin, as well as the world-famous Domaine de la Romanée-Conti – owner of perhaps the most expensive vineyard property in the world.

ALWAYS BACK A WINNER

There aren't any Châteaux in Burgundy because the Dukes of Burgundy supported the losing side in the French Revolution. All the large properties were destroyed and the vineyards were parcelled off to the peasants. Today thousands of different vineyards exist in the region and some of their names have greater prominence on Burgundy labels than the names of the vineyard owners.

- **Côte de Beaune,** surrounding and south of Beaune, produces great red wines (for example, the Pommard and Volnay communes) but is best known for exquisite Chardonnay. The communes of Meursault, Puligny-Montrachet, and Chassagne-Montrachet are where white wines hold court. Here you will find the most prestigious Chardonnay in the world – Le Montrachet Grand Crus.

> **Bargain Districts**
>
> **White wine:**
> Mâconnais;
>
> **Red wine:**
> Côte Chalonnaise,
> Beaujolais-Villages

Côte Chalonnaise, south of Côte d'Or, is an affordable alternative to its expensive neighbours. The communes of Rully, Mercurey, and Givry are worth looking for on wine shop shelves and are best known for their red wines. Montagny and Bouzeron are white wine appellations.

Mâconnais, even farther south, is best known for affordable Chardonnays. It also produces three times more white wine than the whole of Burgundy, so there should be lots of it around. Here you will find the famous and elegant wines of the Pouilly-Fuissé appellation.

Beaujolais, at the very south of Burgundy, produces more than half of the region's wine. This is where the Gamay grape rules.

> *Two, Two, Two Grapes in One*
> **A bottle of Passetoutgrains is made of two-thirds Gamay and one-third Pinot Noir. It's easy drinking, food friendly, and inexpensive.**

An undemanding wine

While Burgundian Pinot Noir and Chardonnay expect so much of wine drinkers, the Gamay grape made into Beaujolais expects nothing. Instead it routinely gives us simple, fresh, fruity, unpretentious, and inexpensive red wines – especially Beaujolais Nouveau. Yet Gamay is also capable of producing more serious and substantial wines. The ten-village crus – including Juliénas, Moulin-à-Vent, Brouilly, Morgon, and Fleurie – produce rich, full-bodied red wines with unique character and the potential to age.

Beaujolais-Villages or Cru Beaujolais is a good, safe bet on a restaurant wine list. It goes well with most foods – even fish and eggs! With its trademark high acidity, low tannin, light body, and low alcohol, Beaujolais is the red wine that thinks it's a white wine. A perfect starter wine.

Georges Duboeuf is one of the most reliable producers in Beaujolais.

The Rhône

The Rhône River winds south from its source in the Swiss Alps before it opens out into the Mediterranean, south of Avignon. The last 250 miles (400 kilometres) or so run through the Rhône wine region – one of the oldest in France.

The Rhône is France's second largest AC wine region; only Bordeaux is bigger. This is serious red wine country: almost 98% of wines produced here are either red or rosé. It is also the region where the international benchmark for Syrah was established.

AC Easy

Compared to Bordeaux and Burgundy, the Rhône's AC structure has three easy-to-understand steps:

- At the bottom is the generic AC Côtes du Rhône. This mainly applies to vineyards in the southern part of the region and covers about 80% of the region's total output. These are good value-priced wines but they aren't meant for serious ageing. Drink up!
- Next are Côtes du Rhône-Villages, a big step up in quality. There are 16 villages, and these may be the best value wines in France. If the actual name of the village appears on the label, it is usually a better wine than the more generic Côtes du Rhône-Villages. Some of the better villages include Rasteau, Visan, Cairanne, and Valréas.
- At the top are the 13 crus – eight in the northern Rhône and five in the south.

A "typical" Rhône wine can be difficult to describe because most Rhône wines are blends – even blends of red grapes and white wine grapes. Neighbouring wines often bear no resemblance to each other.

North vs. South

The Rhône is really two distinct regions: the North – with about 5% of the production and almost all the best wines – and the South, with the rest of the production. (It doesn't get much simpler than that.)

Key Rhône Grapes
Red:
Syrah and Grenache;
White:
Viognier, Marsanne, and
Roussanne

The smaller Northern Rhône is a narrow valley with steep granite slopes. The vines are planted on these slopes, almost defying gravity. Northern Rhône red wines can be quite dense, beefy wines in youth and many take years to come around. Even the white wines, while perfumed and fragrant, are often robust and full bodied. Here are some useful things to know about the Northern Rhône:

- Syrah is the principal red wine grape.
- Viognier is the principal white wine grape. Roussanne and Marsanne are also grown but mainly for blending.
- The top appellations (crus) are Cornas, Hermitage, and Côte-Rôtie. These wines can be pricey: however, Crozes-Hermitage (another cru) offers good-quality wines at a lower price, which are also more widely available.
- The top producers include Paul Jaboulet-Aîné, M. Chapoutier, E. Guigal, and Auguste Clape.

The Southern Rhône, in contrast, is flat and exposed, and highly influenced by the Mediterranean. In a word, it's hot! Southern Rhône wines are much lighter than those from the north. Côtes du Rhône or Côtes du Rhône-Villages wines are good

---

THE POPE'S SUMMER VACATION

Châteauneuf-du-Pape is a wine but it was also the summer home for the Popes in the 14th century, when nearby Avignon, not Rome, was the centre of the Catholic Church. Nowadays, it lends its name to a full-bodied red wine made from a blend of up to 13 different grapes. You will still find the papal coat of arms embossed on every bottle of this wine.

---

entry-level wines for novices and safe bets on a wine list. The region also produces crisp and dry rosé wines that make excellent summer sippers. Here are some useful things to know about the Southern Rhône:

- A wider variety of grapes are planted here, including Syrah, Mourvèdre, Grenache, and Cinsault for the red wines.
- The most notable white wine grape is Muscat, which is used to produce exotic sweet wines like Muscat Beaumes-de-Venise.
- There are five crus; the more notable are Gigondas, Châteauneuf-du-Pape, and Tavel (for rosé). Prices are generally lower in the south, and the wines are also more widely available – especially AC Côtes du Rhône.
- The most famous appellation is Châteauneuf-du-Pape, with the dual distinction of having the highest minimum alcohol strength of any French wine (12.5%) as well as being the first appellation to be regulated under the AC system.
- The top producers include J. Vidal Fleury, Château Rayas, Delas Frères, and Perrin (makers of Château de Beaucastel, Coudoulet de Beaucastel, and the very affordable La Vielle Ferme).

Champagne

Champagne is about 90 miles (145 kilometres) northeast of Paris and is France's northernmost wine region. It is essentially known for one wine – champagne – the most famous sparkling wine in the world. Unlike any other wine, champagne has established itself as a brand name associated with quality, prestige, and celebration. And it has vigorously protected its brand: no other sparkling wine can be called champagne.

The blend's the thing

Champagne is made from Chardonnay or Pinot Noir, or a combination of the two with a little Pinot Meunier thrown in. Because its grapes are grown so far north, the region's wines are usually too thin and acidic to sell on their own. But when made into champagne, they are magically transformed into an elegant wine with millions of tiny, gentle bubbles. The blend of grapes determines the type of champagne:

- *Blanc de Blancs* is made from Chardonnay.
- *Blanc de Noirs* is a white wine made from black grapes – essentially from Pinot Noir and Pinot Meunier.
- *Rosé Champagne* has a *little* red Pinot Noir wine added to the original *cuvée*, or blend.

An Accident Waiting to Happen
Before the 17th century, the wines made in the cold climate of Champagne rarely finished fermenting in the autumn. Fermentation would start up again with the warmth of spring. Since the wines were already in bottles, the second fermentation would create gas and the bottles would explode. Dom Pérignon started looking for a better (and safer) way to contain the bubbles in the wine. The English, who had actually "invented" sparkling wine some 25 years earlier, sold Dom thicker bottles and cork stoppers. The rest, as they say, is history.

Key classifications

Champagne is essentially one appellation. But like all French wine regions, there are some vineyards, crus, that are considered better than others, and these are ranked. Since much of the wines are blends of grapes from different sites, little of this information ends up on the label. Mainly it is used to establish the prices the growers are paid for the grapes.

- There are 38 premier cru vineyards. Krug bottles one famous premier cru – Clos du Mesnil – as a single-vineyard champagne.
- There are 17 grand cru vineyards.

What's Dry?
Champagne can be made dry (extra brut, brut, extra dry), sweet (sec or demi-sec), or extra sweet (doux). One of these words should appear somewhere on the label.

From a consumer's point of view, the main classification to know is the distinction between *vintage* and *non-vintage* champagnes. Vintage champagne is made only in years that are "declared" to be exceptional, and most producers age these wines for a much longer period than their other non-vintage wines.

All champagne corks must have the word champagne stamped on them, and only vintage champagnes can have the year stamped on them. Generally, champagne should be consumed when you buy it. Vintage champagne can keep, but why wait?

Hitting the Marques

Large champagne houses or *Marques* produce champagne in the regional towns of Epernay and Reims. There are about 100 Marques and only a handful of *grandes Marques*. The most famous of the grandes Marques is Möet & Chandon, which makes the renowned *préstige cuvée* called Dom Pérignon.

A bottle of top préstige cuvée will easily break the £50 mark, and some sell for two or three times that amount. However, there are many excellent non-vintage, and even vintage, champagnes selling for much less.

The top Marques include Moët & Chandon, Mumm, Pol Roger, Perrier-Jouët, Piper-Heidsieck, Bollinger, Taittinger, and Veuve Clicquot. Each Marque has a house style based on the grapes in the blend. For example, Pol Roger and Perrier-Jouët are light bodied and elegant while Bollinger and Veuve Clicquot are full bodied and toasty. Try a couple and see which style you prefer.

The Rest of France

We're not finished with France yet. There's more to French wines than just Bordeaux, Burgundy, the Rhône, and Champagne. Here's what to look for from some of the other wine regions.

Alsace

 Alsace is a picturesque region – about 105 miles (170 kilometres) long – in the extreme northeast of France, along its border with Germany. A mixture of French and German traditions flourish in this region and, in fact, mainly Germanic grape varieties are grown. The wines, however, are more French than German – better suited for food, slightly higher in alcohol, and generally drier than their German counterparts. Alsace wines can be a safe bet on a wine list and an ideal choice if you are eating any kind of Asian cuisine.

The Noble Grapes of Alsace
Riesling, Gewürztraminer, Tokay Pinot Gris, and Muscat are the only grape varieties to receive the grand cru designation.

While Riesling is the most planted grape in the region, the exotic Gewürztraminer is the famous grape of Alsace. Pinot Blanc is the second most planted grape, and although it isn't one of the grapes designated as *noble*, it nevertheless produces excellent wine. Gewürztraminer and Pinot Blanc are good starter grapes for exploring the region for the first time. There is renewed interest in Pinot Gris – the grape formerly known as Tokay d'Alsace – as a full-bodied white wine representative of the region. Few Alsace wines need ageing but the better, and sweeter, wines can last for decades.

In Alsace, the grape variety is indicated on the label and AC wines must be bottled in a tall, narrow flûte bottle.

Fantasy Wine
Edelzwicker literally means "noble mixture" in German and is used to describe a blended white wine of two or more noble grape varieties. Winemakers invent fantasy names (e.g., Gentil) for these wines, which will appear on the label. Quality varies but some versions are outstanding.

CLASSY ALSACE WINES
The Alsace classification system is straightforward:

- *Grand Cru* refers to top-rated vineyard sites but not necessarily the top wines. (Some great Alsace wines come from non-rated vineyards.)
- *Vendage Tardive* indicates a late harvest wine made from noble, usually botrytis-affected, grapes. These are usually sweet but they also can be dry.

- *Sélection de Grains Nobles* indicates wines made from selective pickings of botrytis-affected grapes. There's little room for doubt here; these are *very* sweet.

Growers sometimes add other terms like *réserve* or *cuvée exceptionelle* to the label but these don't have any legal standing. These terms usually indicate the winemaker is much more pleased with this wine than in previous vintages.

WHAT TO LOOK FOR

While over 2,000 growers bottle and sell their own wine, this represents slightly less than 20% of the total regional output. About 175 companies bottle the rest. Some of the more reliable and readily available merchants or shippers include Hugel et Fils, Domaine Weinbach, F.E. Trimbach, Léon Beyer, Domaine Marcel Deiss, and Domaine Zind-Humbrecht.

The Loire

The Loire is France's longest river and on its banks are some of the most diverse wine areas in all of France. Its cool maritime climate suggests this is white wine country; however, it is also known for its light, red wines and inexpensive sparkling wines. The influence of the Atlantic decreases as you move inland; as a result, the grapes that are grown in this region, and the wine styles that have developed, are quite different. The region as a whole is best characterized as four subregions:

- *Pays Nantais*, where the River Loire opens to the Atlantic, is known for crisp, dry white wines made from the Muscadet grape.
- *Anjou-Saumur* is best known for its sparkling wine (in Saumur), and some of the world's best sweet wines made from the Chenin Blanc grape (in Anjou).
- *Touraine* is also known for Chenin Blanc (Vouvray), though a drier version, and really good Cabernet Franc (Chinon).
- The *Upper Loire*, or *Centre* as it is sometimes called, includes the famous appellations of Sancerre and Pouilly Fumé. Sauvignon Blanc is the key grape. This is where some of the best goat's cheese is made (Chavignol), which interestingly is a perfect match for Sauvignon Blanc.

The Loire's white wines are crisp and dry and great with food. The reds are light yet elegant and are also food friendly. Better still, they're all affordable so they make good choices on a wine list.

Sur Lie
Muscadet wines may have the words "Sur Lie" appended to their name. This tells you the wine was aged on the lees and bottled straight from the tank. The result is a fresh, crisp, and lively wine with a slight spritz. A great wine to have with steamed mussels.

Chenin Blanc can also be used to make luscious sweet (*moelleux*) wines that can be amazingly long lived. The best sweet wines come from Anjou-Saumur, and two appellations in particular: Quarts-de-Chaume and Bonnezeaux (pronounced *bonzo*).

NO CLASS?

The Loire's wines are classy, and their classification system simple. Just look for the name of the subregion or appellation (e.g., Sancerre) on the label. At last count there were about 60 ACs in total, the most of any wine region in France.

> **Key Grapes**
> White:
> Sauvignon Blanc,
> Chenin Blanc, and
> Muscadet;
> Red:
> Cabernet Franc,
> Pinot Noir

WHAT TO LOOK FOR

In such a large and diverse region, there are many, many producers we could name. Here are a few of our favourites and the AC they are associated with: Henri Bourgeois (Sancerre), Didier Dagueneau (Pouilly-Fumé), Charles Joguet (Chinon), and Domaine de Vieux Chai (Muscadet de Sèvre-et-Maine).

Languedoc-Roussillon

This is the region – often called the Midi – in the south of France that everyone is talking about. Winemakers here have successfully shed years of tradition and inefficiency to produce exciting wines from both traditional and non-traditional grapes. Without the burden of archaic appellation laws, the Old World and the New World seem intent on coming together in the Midi to produce food-friendly, but more importantly, consumer-friendly wines.

Languedoc-Roussillon is the biggest wine region in the world – just over twice as large as Bordeaux. While there are many AC wines from this region, you are more likely to see "vin de pays" on the label and more often than not the grape variety. There are about 100 vin de pays and the largest, Vin de Pays d'Oc, has the better producers. Some of these wines are great and some are not – but they are all good value.

> *Appellations to buy:*
> St-Chinian
> Corbières
> La Clape
> Pic St-Loup
> Fitou

Over 90% of the wine here is red, based on traditional Rhône-style grapes such as Syrah, Grenache, Cinsault, and Mourvèdre, while Carignan is the traditional local choice. Viognier is used for white wine. Like the Rhône, many of the wines are blends. Increasingly, however, the fashionable Cabernet Sauvignon, Merlot, and Chardonnay are being used, and some of these are causing quite a stir.

Putting a Wrap on France

Here are a few other regions you might come across in a local bistro-style restaurant or speciality wine store.

Jura and **Savoie** are two small regions in the east of France bordering Switzerland. Very little gets exported but be on the lookout for the sherry-like curiosity from Jura called Vin Jaune.

Provence is probably best known for its rosé wines and the savoury AC Bandol wine made from the Mourvèdre grape.

The Southwest is often tacked on to Bordeaux, its northern neighbour. This huge area, covering almost all of western France, includes some of the quirkiest wines in the country – full-bodied, tannic monster reds from Cahors and Madiran, Bordeaux-esque beauties from Bergerac and Buzet, and superb sweet wines from Jurançon. This is a region waiting to be discovered. Be the first on your street to try these wines.

ITALY

Many people, when they think of Italian wine, think of Chianti and Soave, and maybe Valpolicella. Trust us, there is much, much more to Italy. Italy is usually in a dead heat with France for the title of leading wine producer worldwide. Vines grow everywhere and wine is an entrenched part of everyday life, along with bread and olive oil.

Italy's white wines tend to be bone-dry, fresh, and neutral while the reds are mouth watering and juicy. The red wines cry out for food while the whites make a perfect apéritif on a hot summer day. Italy also makes big, bold, and ageworthy red wines that are world class in every way.

Wine Classification

1. Piedmont
2. Tuscany
3. Veneto
4. Trentino Alto-Adige
5. Friuli-Venezia Giula
6. Lombardy
7. Emilia-Romagna
8. Umbria
9. Marches
10. Abruzzo
11. Apulia
12. Sicily
13. Sardinia

Like France, Italy controls its wine production; however, the current laws are recent and still changing. Over the past 30 years or so, the Italian wine industry has been in a state of flux, and is only now emerging as a country that consumers can start to trust for quality and consistency.

The first three levels in Italy's classification system are similar to the French system. Perhaps not wanting to be outdone, Italy has one class higher – *Denominazione di Origine Controllata e Garantita* (DOCG). *Vino da tavola* (table wine) and *IGT* (regional wine) represent about 85% of all Italian wine production (compared to less than 50% in France).

There are about 290 DOC (quality wine) regions (compared to over 400 in France). The first wine – Vino

> *Consorzio*
> Each DOC/DOCG zone has a voluntary association called a *consorzio* that offers technical and marketing assistance to its members. Chianti Classico's consorzio is one of the most famous and is represented by the black rooster – the Gallo Nero – on the neck of the bottle.

Nobile di Montepulciano – was promoted to DOCG in 1980, and there are still only 21 wines in this elite category.

But it isn't all that straightforward. Some high-end producers, unhappy with the rigid restrictions placed on them by the system, as well as the different ways the rules and regulations can be interpreted, have chosen to label their wines "Vino da Tavola." These versions, which are some of the best wines in Italy, are expensive and are certainly much higher quality than the classification suggests.

The Italian classification system is not as good an indication of quality as perhaps price is (e.g., not all Chianti Classico DOCG is top quality). Better still, become familiar with some producers.

Regional style

Most of the grapes grown in Italy don't grow anywhere else in the world. While these grapes can be used to make high-quality wine – and many are – they just aren't familiar to most of us.

Over 2,000 grape varieties are grown in Italy, in hundreds of different locations within the 20 wine regions. Even under the DOC system over 900 varieties are approved for production, so it is much more useful to learn about the notable regional styles than grape names.

So how do you navigate through the wine regions of Italy? In a Ferrari would be nice, but here's another way.

Piedmont

Piedmont, which means "at the foot of the mountains," is tucked into the far northwest of Italy. One of Italy's most important and influential wine regions, Piedmont produces one of its most renowned red wines, Barolo. It also produces one of the most fun, Asti.

Piedmont Wines
Red:
Barolo, Barbaresco,
Barbera, and
Dolcetto;
White:
Asti and Gavi

Piedmont is currently home to eight DOCGs and 45 DOCs, the most in Italy. Some of the *denominazione* are named for places (e.g., Barolo or Asti) while others are grape names (e.g., Barbera or Dolcetto). In the case of grape names, a town or commune name is usually affixed to the name of the grape, as in Barbera d'Alba – Barbera from Alba. The denominazione appears on the label.

Long live the King

Barolo – "The Wine of Kings, and King of Wines" – and the less famous Barbaresco, are not grapes but DOCG wines. They are named for the villages, around which the tannic Nebbiolo grapes that make up these wines are grown. Nowhere else in the world does this grape produce such impressive, long-lived wines.

How do Barolo and Barbaresco compare?

- *Barolo* may not look it from its light colour but it's a tannic monster of a wine – lots of acidity with complex and wild aromas of cherries, chocolate, violets, and even truffles (the ones that grow in the ground).
- *Barbaresco* is a similar style, but regulations require less ageing time in the barrel so the wines are usually less full bodied. In most vintages you can usually drink Barbaresco earlier than Barolo.

 Good, traditionally made versions of either wine can be pricey, and don't even think of drinking them until they are 10 years old. Some modern-style producers are making wines for earlier drinking. Reliable producers of Barolo include Elio Altare, Ceretto, Luciano Sandrone, Aldo Conterno, and Giacomo Conterno. For Barbaresco try Gaja, Bruno Giacosa, Castello di Neive, Ceretto, and Marchese di Gressy.

Nebbiolo (which means "little fog") is sometimes called Spanna. Softer, more approachable, and less-expensive Nebbiolo wines come from Langhe and Alba, where the name of the village is affixed to the grape name, and Ghemme and Gattinara, where you will see just the DOC name on the label.

Sweet-tarts

As you get used to drinking Italian wine, you will notice that the hallmark red wine taste is a combination of sweet and tart in the same mouthful. This is the case for two other important grapes in Piedmont, Barbera and Dolcetto.

- *Barbera* has nice acidity and is lighter bodied and lower in tannin than Nebbiolo – mouth watering and easy drinking at the same time.
- *Dolcetto*, which means "the little sweet one," is even juicier and fruitier than Barbera.

Both will age but are better when consumed young and with food. They are often half the price of Barolo or Barbaresco and are definitely ones to look for on a wine list. The grape name often appears on the label or might be added to a place (Barbera d'Alba or Dolcetto d'Alba). Good producers include Ascheri, Luciano Sandrone, Gaja, Aldo Conterno, and Prunotto.

Some wines just gotta have fun

Although Piedmont is famous for its red wine, don't overlook the sparkling wines made, using the tank method, from the Muscat grape. This is Asti country. Noticeably sweet, this wine simply froths in your mouth and has wonderful aromatic qualities. In fact, it actually smells and tastes like grapes. Asti is inexpensive – not bad for a wine that lights up in your mouth.

Herbalicious
Piedmont is also famous for the aromatized wine called vermouth.

Asti is usually sweet and bubbly (*spumante* is the Italian word for sparkling). For fewer bubbles, try Moscato d'Asti. Refreshing and low in alcohol (usually around 5%), it's a great wine to have if you are opening more than one bottle.

Piedmont does have some serious white wines. If you check around you might find some Gavi, made from the Cortese grape. Good versions are usually dry and full bodied, with nice citrus, green apple, and honey aromas.

The Rest of the Northwest

Lombardy is an underrated region, just east of Piedmont, that also makes excellent red wines from the Nebbiolo grape. Lighter bodied and less expensive than Barolo and Barbaresco, these wines are nevertheless gaining an international reputation. The best wines come from the Valtellina DOCG: look for the subdistricts Sassella, Grumello, Inferno, and Valgella on the label. The region also has excellent sparkling wines, made in the classic *méthode traditionelle* style, called Franciacorta DOCG.

The wines of **Val D'Aosta** and **Liguria** are rarely seen as much of it is consumed locally.

Veneto

Veneto may lack the flair of Piedmont, but it too is an important wine region. Tucked into Italy's northeast, around Romeo and Juliet's hometown of Verona, Veneto produces the most recognized white wine in Italy and also one of the more distinguished red wines. It's a safe bet that if Chianti wasn't the first Italian wine you drank, Soave or Valpolicella probably were, or still are.

Veneto is the third largest region in Italy – after Apulia and Sicily – in terms of wine production but the largest in terms of DOC output. It has only one DOCG – a sweet white wine called Recioto di Soave – and 17 DOCs.

> *Key Grapes*
>
> **White:**
> Garganega,
> Trebbiano, and
> Prosecco;
>
> **Red:**
> Corvina, Rondinella,
> and Molinara

Suave Soave

Soave is a bone-dry white wine that doesn't offend; on the other hand, there aren't many versions you'd call memorable. It is made from the fairly average Garganega grape with some undistinguished Trebbiano thrown into the blend. Chardonnay and Pinot Bianco (Pinot Blanc) are now allowed in the blend and add body to these wines.

At its best, Soave has lovely aromas of nuts and honey, and a long lemony finish. Wines from the Classico zone – the older central part of the region – are usually even richer. Anselmi, Bertani, and Pieropan all make good Soave. Masi offers excellent value.

At its worst, Soave can be light but uninteresting – an excellent picnic wine or apéritif. It's best served chilled.

> *Ripasso*
> If you see this on a bottle of Valpolicella, it means the wine has been
> steeped in vats containing the lees of the previous year's Recioto. The
> result is a richer, more full-bodied wine – a mini-Amarone.

Bubbles anyone?

Veneto also has some excellent but underrated dry sparkling wines. They
aren't made from Garganega but rather the Prosecco grape. These are
DOC wines, and you will see the name of the grape on the bottle. Ask
for one next time you want something fizzy.

Valpolicella

The principal red wine grapes of the Veneto region – Corvina,
Rondinella, and Molinara – aren't household names, but the wines they
are blended together to make are. You'll probably recognize them as
Valpolicella and Amarone.

- *Valpolicella DOC* is a light, fruity (cherry), entirely gluggable wine
  that is best when young. These are moderately priced and good picks
  on any wine list. There is also a Valpolicella Classico DOC. Ripasso
  versions are best.
- *Amarone della Valpolicella DOC* (or Amarone for short) is
  made from fully fermented semi-dried (*recioto*) grapes. This
  produces a rich, dry, intense wine, bursting with chocolate
  and dried fruit (plum) aromas, and a long bitter (*amaro* means
  "bitter") almond finish. Amarone has a fairly high alcohol content
  (14–15%). Better versions need five to 10 years ageing.
- *Recioto della Valpolicella* is made like Amarone but is not fermented
  to dryness. The wine, therefore, is slightly sweet and rich, but still has
  that classic bitter finish.

Buying Valpolicella and Amarone rarely ends in
disappointment but it is safer to stick to the top producers:
Allegrini, Boscaini, Tedeschi, Zenato, Tommasi, and
Quintarelli. Masi produces a full range of good-quality Veneto wines, and
at all price ranges.

You can also find good Cabernet Sauvignon, Cabernet Franc, and
Merlot from the eastern part of the region (Piave DOC). The grape
variety may appear on the label.

The Rest of the Northeast

Friuli-Venezia Giula (often just called Friuli for short), just
east of Veneto, has a strong reputation for high-quality, dry
white wines made from local and international grape varieties.
There are eight DOCs and the name of the DOC and/or the grape
variety appears on the label. If you see "colli" on the label that means hill
– wines with a little more character come from these areas.

The Tocai Friulano grape is used to make nutty, full-bodied white
wines, while Ribolla and Verduzzo are even more flavourful and
aromatic. You will also see Pinot Bianco, Chardonnay, Sauvignon Blanc,

and Müller-Thurgau. The red wines are generally lighter in body and flavour. Merlot is the leading grape in terms of production, but the local red grape Refosco makes more interesting wines.

Friuli's most famous wine is a sweet wine called Picolit, made from late harvested or air-dried grapes.

Trentino-Alto Adige is Italy's most northern wine-growing region – on the other side of the Alps from Austria. Due to the cooler climate, this mountainous region is ideal for white wines. In fact, along with Friuli, Alto Adige produces some of Italy's best white wines.

The white wines are generally fresh, light, crisp, and dry. They are excellent with food or just on their own. Usually the label indicates the grape variety. These include Pinot Bianco, Pinot Grigio, Riesling, Gewürztraminer, Chardonnay, Sauvignon Blanc, and Müller-Thurgau. The region also makes excellent sparkling wine around the city of Trento.

Trentino makes red wines from indigenous varieties: Teroldego, Schiava, and Vernatsch. So good are these wines that they rarely make it beyond local consumption.

Emilia-Romagna is better known for its balsamic vinegar, Parma ham, and Parmigiano Reggiano than for its wine. The best-known grape variety here is Lambrusco, which makes light-bodied, thirst-quenching red wines that are low in alcohol and sometimes even slightly fizzy (*frizzante*). Better versions are made in a dry style, unlike the sweet pop-like ones that are often exported.

Tuscany

Probably no region in Italy conjures up more romantic images than Tuscany in central Italy. Its rolling hills and historic towns – Florence, Siena, Montalcino, and San Gimignano – have inspired countless artists, writers, and filmmakers. Here, too, winemaking has been elevated to an art form.

Tuscany is home to six DOCGs, 33 DOCs, and countless premium-quality IGTs, the so-called *Super-Tuscans*. Its most famous red wine is Chianti – a DOCG, as is its oldest zone, Chianti Classico. But Tuscany also produces Brunello di Montalcino – possibly the most expensive DOCG wine in Italy – as well as Vino Nobile di Montepulciano DOCG. Vernaccia di San Gimignano is the only white wine DOCG, and is worth checking out.

Chianti's not a fiasco

You might think of Chianti as pizza wine (some of you may also remember it as that wine that came in the funny straw-wrapped bottle – called a *fiasco*). In the right hands, though, it can be a concentrated and stately wine that can last for decades.

Ricasoli's Legacy
The Chianti blend was created over 130 years ago by Italy's second Prime Minister Baron Ricasoli.

Traditionally, Chianti is a blend and the principal red wine grape in it is Sangiovese. Other grapes – including white wine grapes – are allowed in the Chianti blend but in practice this is rarely done any longer. Nowadays Chianti can be made with 100% Sangiovese.

Like all Italian red wines, Chiantis have that hallmark sweet-tart taste. They are dry, with nice acidity and aromas of cherries, plums, herbs, and even a hint of tobacco or leather. They can be light or even full bodied with a good amount of tannin and a touch of bitterness on the finish.

Chianti is a large region within Tuscany, and is made up of eight subzones. The climate and soils within the region are quite varied and as a result produce wines of different quality and style. Here's a look at what to expect:

- Chianti Classico DOCG is the centre and the oldest part of the Chianti region. Most of the best Chianti comes from here and the black rooster emblem – the Gallo Nero – on the neck of the bottle easily identifies this zone's wines. Producers have to age these wines for a minimum of five years before release. At their best, these are elegant wines, with bright red berry fruit flavours and the characteristic Chianti acidity.
- Chianti DOCG, which surrounds Classico, is made up of the remaining seven subzones. The name of the subzone is usually affixed to the name Chianti (e.g., Chianti Rufina). These wines have to be aged for just over two years before release, but some producers wait longer.
    - Rufina, Colli Fiorentini, and Colli Senesi produce the next highest-rated Chianti – still elegant, with the potential for ageing.
    - The other four – Colli Aretini, Colline Pisane, Montalbano, and Montespertoli – produce lighter, less-distinguished wines meant for early drinking.

In better vintages, producers may hold some Chianti in the barrel longer and offer it as a *riserva*. Tuscany has been enjoying a string of excellent vintages for its red wines since 1997, and there's lots of good Chianti around.

Our favourite Chianti producers include Antinori, Frescobaldi, Fattoria di Felsina, Carpineto, Fontodi, Ruffino, San Felice, Castellare, Fattoria Baggiolino, and Rocca delle Macie.

Big bruisers
The Sangiovese grape is also used in three other important wines in other parts of Tuscany:

- Brunello di Montalcino DOCG, from grapes grown near the town of Montalcino, is an intense, concentrated wine that needs decades before it is ready to drink. Some of the better versions are very expensive. If you are going to spend the money, look for Biondi-Santi, Castelgiocondo, Poggio Antico, or Il Poggione.
- Many Brunello producers also make Rosso di Montalcino DOC. Usually less expensive, these wines are ready-to-drink, lighter versions of their big brothers.
- Vino Nobile di Montepulciano DOCG fits somewhere in between Brunello and Chianti. In good years it can be almost as powerful as Brunello, yet elegant like Chianti. Look for Avignonesi or Carpineto.

> ### Vin Santo
> Vin Santo is a traditional Tuscan dessert wine made from air-dried grapes. The sweet juice ferments slowly and matures for as many as five to six years – bellissimo!

Super-Tuscans

Many Tuscan producers make prestige wines by blending the local Sangiovese grape with non-traditional grapes, like Cabernet Sauvignon and Merlot, or make wines from these international varieties alone. Because these grapes are not allowed under the current rules, or the wines were produced outside the Chianti zone, they don't qualify as DOC or DOCG. In protest, producers simply label their wines vino da tavola or IGT. Some of these wines (e.g., Sassicaia) were recently awarded their own DOC status, but will others follow?

Super-Tuscans aren't cheap: some command price tags well over £40. They usually bear a proprietary name, like Solaia, Tignanello, and Ornellaia. The style of these world-class wines varies depending on the grapes in the blend and the producer. Some are Chianti-like while others are more New World.

What Else is in the Middle?

Umbria is best known for the widely exported dry white wine called Orvieto. Made from the Trebbiano grape, these are usually bland wines. Stick with the better producers (Bigi) or the Classico versions.

 Red wines to watch for include the Chianti-like Torgiano DOC – better known as Rubesco (made only by Lungarotti) – or the rich and intense Sagrantino di Montefalco DOCG.

Marches is world famous for its grape Verdicchio, or, rather, the green amphora-shaped bottle the wine is sold in. Don't think this is just pretty packaging – the dry white wine inside is pretty good.

Lazio, also known as Latium, is where Rome is located. It is best known for a white wine called Frascati DOC, made from Malvasia and Trebbiano. Some versions have character (the ones with more Malvasia) but many are simply bland.

Abruzzo's claim to fame is the inexpensive Montepulciano d'Abruzzo. This low tannin, easy-drinking red wine is a favourite of banquet halls. It has nothing to do with the town of the same name, however, which is in Tuscany.

Molise wines are rarely exported, and for many years it didn't even have any DOC wines. The beefy red wine called Biferno DOC is one to watch for.

The South

This is currently where the action is in Italy. Some of the more exciting Italian red wines are being produced here, and stepped-up investment in the wineries means the quality is improving, too. The climate is reliable, so vintages aren't really an issue. You will consistently get good-value wines with unrestrained flavour.

Puglia (Apulia)

This region is the "heel" of Italy's "boot." Wine has been produced here for over 4,000 years and more wine is produced in this area than anywhere else in Italy. But it isn't just about quantity: there are some great-quality wines here, too (though less than 10% of Puglia's wines are DOC quality). The better wines come from the Salento peninsula: Salice Salentino, Copertino, and Squinzano.

Get acquainted with wines made from the grape called Negroamaro (meaning "bitter black"), because everyone is going to be talking about it soon. It makes deep, rich, and flavourful wines that can take five or so years to come around. These wines are a real bargain.

Primitivo – long thought to be the same grape as Zinfandel – as well as international grape varieties like Chardonnay are also grown in this region.

Sicily

The island of Sicily is probably best known for the fortified wine known as Marsala. It is a hot region, so the better wines come from the higher elevations near the middle of the island. Here the Nero d'Avola grape makes excellent full-bodied, intense red wines. On an island off the Sicilian coast – Pantelleria – you will find lovely fortified dessert wines made from the Moscato (Muscat) grape.

Campania, Basilicata, and Calabria

We simply don't see a lot of wines from these three regions. Campania has a slight lead on the others with the soft and delicate dry white wine called Greco di Tufo DOC and the more aromatic, hazelnutty Fiano di Avellino DOC. The plummy red wine called Taurasi DOC also makes it to our shores.

Sardinia

While not actually in the south, the island of Sardinia is gaining a reputation for excellent red wines made from the Cannonau grape, the Italian name for the Grenache grape. DOC versions are aged in oak and the name of the grape appears on the label.

GERMANY

Compared to France and Italy, or many other countries for that matter, Germany is rarely considered to be a winemaking powerhouse or even a wine-drinking culture. It ranks seventh in terms of wine production and only 13th when it comes to per capita wine consumption (the average German drinks about eight times more beer than wine). So why does Germany merit coverage right behind Italy?

In our opinion it is because Germany gives us some of the best white wines in the world. And they do so in conditions so extreme – many of the vineyards lie as far north as grapes will ripen and on terrain almost as inhospitable – that you wonder how this is possible. German wine may seem unfashionable (sweet isn't "in" at the moment) and, judging by the labels, even out of step from the rest of the world; nevertheless, these wines are begging to be discovered.

It's Riesling

There's only one grape to worry about – Riesling. It represents about 25% of production. Even on the most gothic labels, the word Riesling will show up somewhere on the bottle.

German Riesling is low in alcohol (less than 10% for drier wines), has nice acidity, smells fruity (green apple, apricot, or peach) and sometimes minerally or smoky when young. It can be made in a range of styles from dry to lusciously sweet. When it ages, Riesling acquires a highly prized quality – an aroma reminiscent of petrol.

About 20% of Germany's 2,600 vineyards are planted with the early-ripening Müller-Thurgau. This grape is used to make lower-priced blends and is the main ingredient in most Liebfraumilch. Red wine grapes make up about 20% of production and the leading grape is Pinot Noir (called Spätburgunder – "late" Burgundy).

Germany is also known for a value-priced sparkling wine called Sekt.

It's Not Only Sweet

Forty percent of all German wines are actually produced *trocken* (dry) or *halbtrocken* (off dry). The trend now is to use these words on the label so it's easier to pick them out.

But the real secret to quality German wines is their hallmark acidity. Even a halbtrocken wine seems drier when balanced with acidity. And as foodies know, this makes German wines probably the most food friendly of all white wines, or at least the most versatile.

It's All on the Label

German wine laws may appear to be the most complex in the world – and the confusing labelling doesn't help, either – but once you learn the basics, they are probably the most consumer friendly. Everything you need to know is on the label.

German wines are classified according to the sugar content – or must weight – of the grapes at harvest (called the *Prädikat*), not after they are made into wine, as is the case in most other countries. In any given year, in theory, any vineyard location is capable of producing high-quality wine, and many do. More than 90% of wine produced in Germany is in the quality category.

At the bottom of the scale are *Tafelwein* and *Landwein*. Next is *Qualitätswein bestimmter Anbaugebeite* or QbA for short. In English this means a "quality wine from a particular area or region." It's not really "quality" wine; natural ripeness levels are usually so low that these wines are routinely chaptalized (sugar is added during fermentation).

Qualitätswein mit Prädikat or QmP is where it gets interesting. In

English, QmP means, "quality wine with special attributes." In cooler years, not much QmP wine is made, as the grapes haven't ripened enough. In warmer years, production is higher. QmP wines are considered better wines because the grapes have to be fermented as harvested, and no sugar can be added.

QmP wines are further classified into six levels, but you'll probably encounter only the first three:

- *Kabinett* wines are the lightest of the QmP wines with an often-perfect balance of sweetness and acidity. There aren't any limits on sugar levels or alcohol content in the finished wine so these wines can be dry or off dry, but never sweet. The best Kabinett wines come from the Mosel or Nahe regions.
- *Spatlese* means "late harvest." The grapes are more mature at harvest than Kabinett grapes, so the wines are fuller. Spatlese wines are generally made in a sweeter style, and the best dry versions come from the Pfalz and Baden regions.
- *Auslese* means "selected harvest." These wines are made from grapes that have started to shrivel up or have been botrytized. They are rarely made dry and are the more expensive of the three levels.

If you want even sweeter wines, then look for "Beerenauslese," "Eiswein" (icewine), or "Trockenbeerenauslese" on the label. Only the most mature grapes have been fermented for these wines and they will be sweet and expensive.

German wines are bottled in the traditional tall, narrow flûtes, with one exception: the wines that come from the Franken region.

Focus on Four

Since the re-unification of Germany, there are 13 wine regions (called *Anbaugebeit*). You need to know just four:

- *The Pfalz* is the biggest region in terms of production and has some of the most interesting and exciting wines. Some of the most famous estates include Bürklin-Wolf, von Buhl, and Müller-Catoir.
- *The Mosel-Saar-Ruwer* is really three regions. The vines are grown on the steep slopes of the rivers of the same name. The region produces a lot of average wine but is also home to some of Germany's most famous vineyards (called *Einzellagen*). Mosel wines are bottled in green bottles, as opposed to the more commonly seen brown bottles.
- *The Nahe*, while eclipsed by the other regions in terms of production, makes classic Riesling of distinction and elegance.
- *Baden*, the most southerly wine region, is the region on the rise. There is a lot of modernization taking place in the wineries and we will see more of these wines in the future.

The other regions are Ahr (known for red wines despite being Germany's most northerly wine region), Franken (known for dry white wines made from the Silvaner grape), Rheinhessen (this is Liebfraumilch country), Württemberg (known for red wines), Hessische Bergstrasse, Mittelrhein, Saale-Unstrut, and Sachsen.

Using Your Words

It is easy to be confused by German wine labels as so many of them are intricately designed and the type is often hard to read (though we find that this is changing). Here's what else you need to know:

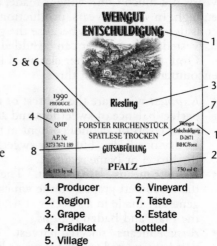

- The name of the region will always appear on the label, either at the bottom or top, or prominently written in the middle if it's QbA wine.
- If it is a QmP wine, immediately after or below the vintage you'll see the name of the district (*Bereiche*), village (*Gemeind*), or group of vineyards (*Grosslage*), followed by the name of the

1. Producer	6. Vineyard
2. Region	7. Taste
3. Grape	8. Estate
4. Prädikat	bottled
5. Village	

vineyard (*Einzellage*). The first word will have "-er" affixed to it, meaning it's "from" that place. For example, *Forster Pechstein* indicates the grapes are from the vineyard called Pechstein, near the village of Forst.
- Elsewhere on the label you'll find the producer's name, the grape variety, the Prädikat if it's a QmP wine, and perhaps the sweetness level in the finished wine. If it doesn't say "trocken," assume it is sweet.

Buying Tips

- Stay with the regions we've mentioned and the style of wine you like, and you won't go far wrong.
- Look for wines with QmP on the label; they are only slightly more expensive but you'll have a good idea of what you are getting. Germany has enjoyed five strong vintages since 1994 (except 1998), so there should be a lot of QmP wine around.
- Buy from trusted producers: Selbach-Oster, J.J. Prüm, Dr. Bürklin-Wolf, Müller-Catoir, Reichsgraf Von Kesselstatt, Reichsrat von Buhl, Kurt Darting, and Balbach.

SPAIN

Despite having more land under vine than any other country, Spain's reputation for quality wine has left a lot to be desired. But recently a sort of wine renaissance has hit Spain; Spanish wine, like the country's food, is becoming popular again.

The image of musty old wines is being pushed aside by a desire to produce clean, modern wines. Producers are experimenting with international grape varieties and advanced winemaking techniques. The results of this transition have been nothing short of amazing. Spain produces some lovely juicy, gluggable red wines, and fresh, clean, dry white wines that can give the rest of Europe, and even the New World, a run for its money. It is also producing wines that can last for decades, if you're patient enough.

The number one grape in terms of worldwide production – Airén – is native to Spain. Very little of it ends up as wine; it is mainly used in the production of Spanish brandy. Spain's better wines are made from local grapes like Tempranillo, Garnacha, Verdejo, and Albariño, but increasingly, international varieties like Cabernet Sauvignon and Chardonnay are being added to the mix.

Spain's biggest climate problem is lack of rain. Some parts of the country are the driest in Europe. Since irrigation has been allowed, beginning in 1996, Spain has enjoyed a run of good vintages.

Spain's Wines Are Classified

Spain's system resembles Italy's, including the *Denominación de Origen e Calificada* (DOCa) for the highest category of wines. So far only one region – Rioja – has been awarded this distinction.

The system seems simple enough, except Spanish wines also have ageing requirements. These requirements (the amount of time the wine has to stay in the barrel and bottle) apply to both white and red wines, though red wines usually have longer requirements. There are some variations across the regions – most notably Rioja – but this is what the following words mean on the label:

- *Crianza* wines meet the minimum ageing requirements. Crianza are usually pleasant, light-bodied wines that are drinkable right away.
- *Reserva* wines usually spend one to two more years ageing than crianza wines, and the better wines have probably been aged even longer. Reserva are usually very good wines and the ones to search out.
- *Gran reserva* wines are allowed only in the best vintages and have even longer ageing requirements. As a result, the prices are usually higher.

Of Spain's 17 regions, only 13 have DO (quality) wines, and only seven of those produce wines of note. The name of the region, however, is not as important as the area of production (DO) – that's what will appear on the label.

Spain is rapidly developing its classification system. Currently there are about 55 DOs and one DOCa. Most of the best wine production takes place north of Madrid (though Andalucía, where sherry comes from, is in the south).

Rioja

One of the most traditional wine regions in Spain, Rioja has recently undergone major changes in terms of its style. As a result, the rustic, oaky, thin style that featured characteristic vanilla and strawberry aromas is being replaced by deep, refreshing, and juicy wines. A more modern, international profile is emerging.

Red Rioja wines are mainly made from Tempranillo grapes, with Garnacha and some other local varieties in the blend. In keeping with Old World traditions, it's the name of the region, however, that appears on the label.

White Riojas are made from the local Viura grape. Modern versions are crisp, neutral, and inoffensive, while traditional versions are bold and flavourful.

Rioja producers to look for include Marqués de Riscal, Marqués de Murrieta, Castillo Ygay, and Artadi.

Ribera del Duero

This region also uses Tempranillo grapes (known here as Tinto Fino) for its red wines and often they are richer and more elegant wines than in Rioja. Its three most famous producers are Vega Sicilia – whose wine Unico is aged longer than any other red wine in the world and never released before 10 years after the harvest – Dominico de Pingus, and Pesquera de Duero, but there is usually a fair amount of Ribera around from other producers. This is a region to watch.

Navarra

Located just above Rioja, this region used to be famous only for its rosé (rosado) wines made from the Garnacha grape. Now it produces exciting red wines from (sometimes over-oaked) international grapes (Cabernet Sauvignon is often used in the blend). Some of these wines can give Rioja a run for its money. Lots of innovation and experimentation suggest this is also a region to watch. Chivite and Guelbenzu are reliable producers.

Penedés

Best known for its sparkling wine called Cava, this is also the region where the internationally recognized producer Torres is based. Torres wines are some of the best value, well-made wines coming out of Spain at the moment. Many of the region's wines are made from easily recognizable international grape varieties, and the names appear right on the labels.

The Rest of Spain

In the rest of Spain, **Priorat** is one of the rising stars. The region produces spicy, full-bodied wines that are in high demand, with prices to match. **Rueda**, in the historic Castilla Y León region, makes wonderfully crisp, aromatic white wines from the native Verdejo and Viura grapes. And **Rías Baixas** (REE-as by-shuss) is the home of an elegantly aromatic white wine made from the Albariño grape.

OTHER OLD WORLD COUNTRIES

France, Italy, Spain, and Germany together make up over 80% of Europe's production (and over half of total world production), which is why they deserved the extra attention. The wines from these four countries are the ones most likely to show up on restaurant wine lists and wine shop shelves. But what about the other Old World countries – what do you need to know about them? Here are the other wine regions you might come across in your local supermarket, and what to expect if you pick up a bottle of their wine.

Portugal

Portugal is famous for its fortified wines, port and madeira, as well as the rosé Mateus. However, Portugal also produces good red and white table wines, albeit from lesser-known local varieties. The better red wines come from the regions of **Douro, Dão**, and **Bairrada**. While these wines have been traditionally rustic and overly tannic, recent advances in winemaking have resulted in wines that are more appealing to international palates. Give one a try with a meal and you'll see what we mean.

Portugal's most distinctive white wine is the ubiquitous **Vinho Verde** DOC. Bone dry, this wine is fairly aromatic (think peaches) with a piercing acidity and a little "spritz" on the finish. Not for keeping; drink this wine as soon as you buy it.

Hungary

Hungary is making a name for itself on the international scene. No longer wishing to be solely reliant on its full-bodied Egri Bikaver (which means "bull's blood from Eger") or the softer and spicier Szekszárdi, producers started to plant international varieties and you can now find many good-value examples of Chardonnay and Pinot Gris. Hungary has a lot of potential – especially with native varieties like Kadarka, Kékfrancos, Furmint, and Irsai Olivér – and recent investments in the wineries mean we can expect more and better things to come.

Coverage of Hungary would be incomplete without a mention of Tokaji Aszú, in particular Essencia, one of the world's best sweet wines.

Greece

Winemaking as we know it started in Greece. Despite its lineage, however, Greece hasn't kept up with the times and it's only in the past 15 years or so that its wines have begun to take their place on the international stage. Most people still think of Retsina (a wine flavoured with pine resin) when they think of Greece. This is unfortunate as Greeks now make some excellent full-bodied red and tangy white wines using native varieties, from appellations like **Naoussa**, **Nemea**, and **Zitsa**, as well as the sweet liqueur wines (made from dried Muscat and Mavrodaphne grapes) from Patras.

Austria

Austria is a small wine-producing country – it doesn't make the top 20 – but it produces some very good wines. Like Germany, Austria is white wine country. It has a similar classification system (with a couple of exceptions); however, the wines themselves have more alcohol and body and are generally drier.

The leading grape is Grüner Veltliner, which can make excellent dry and off-dry white wines. The best come from **Niederösterreich** (lower Austria), **Wachau**, which also produces very nice wines made from Riesling, and **Kremstal**.

Eastern Europe

The wine world seems to be rushing to discover the wines of Bulgaria, Romania, Czech Republic, Slovakia, Slovenia, and the Balkan States. These countries are emerging as sources of good, inexpensive wines if you are selective. Ask a trusted wine shop for advice before grabbing a £3 bottle of Laski Rizling from Velika Morav.

Bulgaria is probably the safest bet right now – especially for Merlot and Cabernet Sauvignon – but don't count out Romania (the eighth largest wine-producing region, behind Germany). Increased investment in the former Soviet Republics may also mean we'll be seeing more quality wine from places like Moldova, Georgia, Azerbaijan, and Russia in the future.

England

Due to its cooler climate, you might be surprised to learn that England produces wine at all. England is, however, developing somewhat of a reputation especially for its sparkling wines, which is interesting given its invention of the wine in the first place.

The countryside is dotted with hundreds of vineyards, mainly in the southern counties of Sussex, Kent, Surrey, Hampshire, Devon and Cornwall. Many of the vineyards have visitor centres and run tours and their wines are now being stocked in supermarkets and wine shops – look out for Camel Valley, Three Choirs, Wickham, Lamberhurst, Tenterden (Curious Grape and Chapel Down), Breaky Bottom, Nyetimber, Ridge View and Denbies.

Go on line
To find a full list of all the English vineyards check out
www.countrylovers.co.uk and www.englishwineproducers.com

Switzerland

Not much is exported from Switzerland, the best being the dry white wines made in the French style, from the Chasselas grape. There's an enjoyable Swiss red wine called Dôle – a blend of Gamay and Pinot Noir – and in the Italian-speaking part of Switzerland (Ticino) they make very good Merlot.

> *We're Number 1*
> Tiny Luxembourg has the highest per capita wine consumption in the world.

Eastern Mediterranean Countries

The eastern Mediterranean – called the Levant – is thought to be where wine was first made. Grapes are still important to this region, but not necessarily for making wine (Turkey, for example, is the fifth-largest producer of grapes in the world but most of them are for eating.) Cyprus is best known for its fortified wine Commandaria, and Tunisia, Israel, and Lebanon export wines to North America but in small amounts. Most remarkable is Lebanon's internationally renowned Château Musar, which makes a Bordeaux-like blend from Cabernet Sauvignon and Cinsault.

UNITED STATES

Outside Europe, the United States is the most important wine producer in the world. It ranks fourth in the world in terms of wine production – about half of what France and Italy each produce – but is the technological leader in both grape growing and winemaking. While it was the Roman historian Pliny the Elder who wrote *in vino veritas* – in wine there is truth – it was probably a Californian winemaker who coined the phrase *in vino monetas* – in wine there is money.

The U.S. is one of the few New World countries to classify its wine production. In 1983, it adopted an appellation system (American Viticultural Areas or AVAs) to define the geographical boundaries of the wine areas. Currently, there are about 145 AVAs, in 27 states, and more than half of them (86) are in California.

The AVA system doesn't work the way European classification systems do. There are no rules concerning what grapes can be grown in which AVA, or how the wine is made. You might have to experiment a little to find the grape, style, or producer you like.

> *Napa Not First*
> The first AVA was not awarded to California but to Augusta, Missouri, in 1990. Napa was awarded AVA status three years later.

The federal government also imposed guidelines to bring some honesty to wine labelling. The wine must now include at least 75% of the grape variety identified on the label, and 85% if it's an AVA wine.

> *States to Look For*
> Arizona, Idaho, Missouri, Texas, and Virginia

Membership Has Its Privileges
Meritage is the trademarked name for American wine made with grapes of the traditional Bordeaux blends – red and white. Wines wishing to use this name must be part of the Meritage Association and are subject to its rules.

By some reports there are wineries in 46 of the 50 states. The most notable, in terms of quality wine production, are in California, Oregon, Washington, and New York. In the other states, with a few exceptions, most vineyards are planted with cold-hardy French hybrids or native *Vitis labrusca* vines. Depending on where you live, availability from certain state wineries may be limited. For example, don't expect to see the wines from Valiant Vineyards – South Dakota's oldest winery – everywhere just yet.

California

California put the United States on the world map with respect to wine. Much of the credit goes to the brothers Gallo – Ernest and Julio – who, after Prohibition ended, built the world's largest wine-producing company, known for its inexpensive "jug" wines (Hearty Burgundy) and now for a line of premium-quality wines from Sonoma. Robert Mondavi also should receive credit. Mondavi's dedication to quality has earned him the international respect of his peers as well as domestic success. Stag's Leap's Cabernet Sauvignon beating top Bordeaux in a blind tasting in the early 1970s didn't hurt the image of California wines, either!

While there are many different grape varieties grown in California, the major classic Bordeaux and Burgundy varieties – Cabernet Sauvignon, Chardonnay, and Pinot Noir – are favoured for quality wines, albeit with a distinct Californian style. Stylistically, the emphasis is on BIG – there is nothing subtle about Californian wine. It's all about ripe, fruit-driven character.

- *Cabernet Sauvignon* is intense, sweet blackberry and plum fruit with ample tannins and vanilla oak.
- *Pinot Noir* has bright cherry fruit flavour, sometimes jammy, with nice, elegant structure.
- *Chardonnay* is ripe, sweet fruit, with toasty and buttery qualities from the oak.

Other grape varieties include Zinfandel – which is used to make fruity, gluggable wines as well as hearty, peppery wines with lots of bramble fruit – and Sauvignon Blanc; Rhône grapes like Syrah, Grenache, and Viognier; and even Italian grapes like Sangiovese. The climate is so conducive to grape growing that pretty well everything can grow, though perhaps not as well as in its home country.

California produces an incredible range of wines, from inexpensive "jug" wines to pricey "cult" wines. Expect to pay a lot more for *reserve* and vineyard-selected wines from the best AVAs and producers. In general, only the best wines improve with age, so it's a good idea to drink Californian wine right away.

Vintage variation is not much of a problem in California, and it has had a string of excellent vintages recently. Pretty much anything from 1996 on is worth buying.

Napa Valley

Napa Valley isn't the state's largest wine-producing area but it produces the majority of California's prestigious wines, the most important of which are Chardonnay and Cabernet Sauvignon. In a supporting role you'll also find Sauvignon Blanc (Fumé Blanc), Merlot, Zinfandel, and Pinot Noir (from the Carneros AVA).

Temperatures can vary by as much as 10°F (6°C) along the valley's 30 mile (45 kilometre) length. That means there can be a considerable difference between wines grown in the cooler Carneros (in the south) and those in the much warmer Calistoga (in the north). Many of the better AVAs are located at higher altitudes, away from the burning heat of the valley floor. Diamond Creek, Spring Mountain, Stag's Leap, Howell Mountain, and Rutherford are examples of excellent AVAs.

While there are far too many excellent Napa producers to list, here are a few you might want to try: Robert Mondavi, Chateau Montelena, Clos du Val, Clos Pegase, Duckhorn, Robert Pecota, Beringer, and Whitehall Lane.

There are also many excellent sparkling wine producers in Napa (though some are actually in the Carneros region, south of Napa) including Domaine Chandon, Schramsberg, Cordoniu Napa, Mumm Napa Valley, and Domaine Napa.

Sonoma County

Sonoma County has a large number of microclimates, especially cooler ones. This has allowed Pinot, Zinfandel, and Sauvignon Blanc to take centre stage. Some of the best Pinot Noir outside Burgundy comes from Sonoma, particularly from the cooler Russian River Valley AVA. Dry Creek Valley AVA – where Gallo is a major presence – is especially good for Zinfandel. Other notable AVAs include the warmer Alexander Valley and Knight's Valley.

Sonoma originally had a better reputation for fine wine than Napa, but Napa has taken the lead in recent years. There are still many excellent producers including Chateau St. Jean, Gary Farrell, Paul Hobbs Cellars, Ravenswood, Sonoma-Cutrer, Buena Vista, Gundlach-Bundschu, and Marimar Torres.

Bay Area

Just south of San Francisco are a couple of areas worth noting. On the east side of the Bay is **Livermore**. Here you will find excellent white wines, most notably Sauvignon Blanc. Look for Wente Bros., one of the area's oldest wineries.

Santa Cruz Mountains has attracted some of the best and most eclectic winemaking in the state. Chardonnay, Cabernet, and Pinot do well here. Bonny Doon Vineyards – led by iconoclastic owner Randall Grahm – routinely pushes accepted winemaking practices – for example, by emphasizing Rhône grapes in their wines, or coming up with highly original marketing ideas. In addition to irreverent wine names and labels, the wines are always worth seeking out. Other notable Santa Cruz producers include David Bruce, Bargetto, and Ridge Vineyards.

Further south, **Monterey County** is starting to make a name for itself with Chardonnay. Look for Chalone and Robert Talbott.

Central Coast

Closer to Los Angeles is an area called the Central Coast. The wineries in this area haven't yet achieved the status of Napa and Sonoma; nevertheless, they produce excellent wines.

San Luis Obispo is really two distinct districts: the hotter **Paso Robles** and the cooler **Edna Valley** and **Arroyo Grande**. Paso Robles is best known for its Zinfandel, while Pinot Noir and Chardonnay do better in Edna Valley. Rhône varieties are also grown here. Producers to look for include Meridian, Corbett Canyon, Castoro Cellars, Tablas Creek, J. Lohr, and Talley.

Santa Barbara's best wines come from the still cooler **Santa Maria Valley** and **Santa Ynez Valley** AVAs. Here they excel with Chardonnay and Pinot Noir. Top producers include Au Bon Climat, Firestone, Gainey, Richard Longoria, Sanford, and Lane Tanner.

Oregon

Oregon vineyards are west of the Cascade Mountains, where the climate is cool and damp. Good weather isn't reliable so there is considerable variation between vintages. In the past five years, only 1996, 1998, and 1999 can be considered good vintages.

Oregon is suited to Burgundian grape varieties and Pinot Noir is the star. Chardonnay is the second most planted grape but is being rapidly replaced by Pinot Gris, which makes more interesting wines. Oregon wines are more European (lighter and more subtle) than Californian in style.

The state has six AVAs. The **Willamette Valley** is the most important, where most of the best Pinot Noir is grown and many of the more celebrated producers are located: Adelsheim, Amity, Erath, and The Eyrie Vineyards. Also look for Cameron, Domaine Drouhin, St. Innocent, Sokol Blosser, and Ponzi.

WINE PIONEER

In 1970, David Lett, ower and winemaker of The Eyrie Vineyards, released the first Pinot Noir from Oregon. David had the insight and courage to believe that world-class Pinot Noir could be made in Oregon. The rest, as they say, is history.

Washington State

Washington State vineyards are mostly east of the Cascades and the climate is semi-arid, even desert-like. The weather is more reliable than Oregon's and vintages are consistently good. Washington has enjoyed an unbroken string of excellent vintages since 1996.

Bordeaux grapes (Cabernet and Merlot) produce big, rich, flavourful wines with considerable ageing potential. Syrah is also doing well here. White wines don't have the profile of the reds, but there are good Chardonnays as well as Sauvignon Blanc and Sémillon.

Washington has five AVAs. **Walla Walla Valley** is where most of the premium wineries are found. Look for Chateau Ste. Michelle, Canoe Ridge, Columbia Crest, L'Ecole #41, Hedges Cellars, The Hogue Cellars, Leonetti, and Woodward Canyon.

New York State

Grapes have been grown in New York State for over 150 years. It is the third-largest region in the United States and is home to its second largest wine company, Canandaigua.

Like Niagara to its west, New York is a cool climate grape-growing region. Although it is better suited to white wine grapes, it also produces some impressive red wines. Riesling does very well, as do French hybrids like Vidal and Seyval Blanc. As for the reds, Merlot and Pinot Noir do well in good vintages. There is a lot of vintage variation.

The state has a total of seven AVAs. **Finger Lakes, Hudson River Valley**, and **Long Island** are the most important. While New York has a long tradition with winter-hardy French hybrid grapes, the Finger Lakes AVA produces excellent white wines from international varieties (including Chardonnay), and the milder Long Island AVAs are gaining stride with red varieties including Cabernet Sauvignon, Merlot, and Cabernet Franc.

CANADA

Canada is a small wine-growing country, but there is nothing small about its attitude toward making and selling world-class wine. Canada produces excellent wines, including its now famous icewine, though much of it is consumed domestically.

Most of the country is above the 50th parallel, outside the ideal range of production for grapes. And while Canada's Niagara region is on the same latitude as Tuscany, here the similarity ends. Canada is a cool climate wine-growing region with a much shorter growing season.

Vinland

It is believed that the Viking Leif Ericsson landed somewhere on Canada's east coast around 1000 AD and found so many vines growing that he named his discovery Vinland (Land of Wine).

There are wineries in only four of Canada's 10 provinces (Nova Scotia, Quebec, Ontario, and British Columbia) and most of the best quality wines currently come from Ontario and British Columbia.

MEXICO

Don't be surprised if Mexico doesn't spring to mind as a wine-producing country. Tequila or cervezas are probably what you think of first. But actually Mexico was the starting point for grape growing in the Americas some 400 years ago.

While much of the country is simply too hot for growing grapes, the cooler North Baja Peninsula – just over the border from San Diego – and the higher altitude Querétaro region have proved to be well suited to the task. Here traditional French varietals like Chardonnay, Merlot, Cabernet Sauvignon, and Pinot Noir do well. Some Californian varietals like Zinfandel and Petite Sirah have also adapted well, as has Nebbiolo.

Although there are some quality-driven, boutique-style wineries, Mexico also produces value-priced wine in relatively large quantities. Mexican wines can have a rustic, jammy quality so find a producer you like – LA Cetto and Monte Xanic are good bets – and stick with them.

SOUTH AMERICA

The strong European influence of South America's immigrants has helped shape a wine industry based on international varietals. And if you are looking for good value, look no further. Stricter controls on labelling (what it says on the label is now what's inside the bottle!) and huge investments in upgrading production facilities have helped this region gain a substantial share of the market in North America – if not the world. It doesn't hurt that many good wines from South America are inexpensive. Quality, flavour, and value – what more can you ask for?

Six of the 13 South American countries produce wine. Brazil used to be the fourth-largest wine-producing country in the world but has slipped considerably in recent years. Uruguay makes good wines, including the beefy and tannic Tannat, but they rarely are found outside the country. For now, the countries you're most likely to see represented on the shelves are Chile and Argentina.

Chile

Currently the 11th-largest producer of wine in the world, Chile is regarded as the leading producer of fine wine in South America. Its near-perfect climate and recent political and economic stability indicate this is a wine country on the move.

There are 5 main growing regions:

- **Aconcagua**, which includes the Casablanca subregion, produces excellent red and white wines.
- **Maipo** is the most famous region and where most of the wineries are located. Cabernet and Chardonnay do well, as do Merlot and Sauvignon.

No Louse Here!
Chile is one of the only countries in the world that is phylloxera-free. The combination of sandy soil and geographic isolation has kept the vineyards uncontaminated. As a result, Vitis vinifera vines grow on their own rootstocks. Many of the vines are therefore older than their counterparts in the rest of the world, and can produce better fruit.

- **Rapel** includes the famous Colchagua subregion, where Cabernet Sauvignon is the most-planted grape variety. Rapel has a reputation for full-flavoured red wines.
- **Maule** and **Bío-Bío** are the more southerly and cooler regions.

Chile is best known for juicy, gluggable red wines. The fruit is consistently ripe and winemakers are not afraid to show it. Although many Chilean wines are inexpensive, a number of premium-priced red wines are being produced, including some joint ventures with European and U.S. winemakers. These wines can age, but most Chilean wines should be drunk right away.

Key Grapes

Red:
Merlot, Cabernet Sauvignon, and Pinot Noir;

White:
Chardonnay and Sauvignon Blanc

Chilean white wines, on the other hand, lack fruit flavour intensity because of overly enthusiastic irrigation or over cropping. Stick with cooler regions, Casablanca in particular, to be sure of quality.

Chilean wine labels indicate the grape and usually the region. The climate is not variable so vintages are not an issue. You should always find inexpensive but good Merlot and Cabernet on the shelves of your supermarket. But hurry, prices keep going up! It's also a good idea to find a few producers you can trust: Santa Rita, Santa Carolina, Undurraga, Los Vascos, Concha y Toro, and Casa Lapostolle.

Argentina

Argentina ranks fifth in the world in terms of production. Most of the wine is consumed locally: Argentineans consume more wine per capita than any other country except tiny Luxembourg and Spain. There is really only one wine region of note – **Mendoza**. However, **Salta** and **Rio Negro** are also quickly developing reputations for good wine.

Like Chile, this is red wine territory but with a completely different range of grapes. Everyone in the New World uses Cabernet Sauvignon and Merlot, but only Argentina makes great soft and juicy wine from Malbec (its leading-quality grape variety). It also works with Italian varieties – Barbera, Bonarda (its most-planted red wine grape), and Sangiovese – and Spanish varieties like Tempranillo and Syrah.

White wine production is taken less seriously in Argentina, with the exception of wines made from the wonderfully aromatic Spanish grape Torrontés. Other white grape varieties include Chenin Blanc, Chardonnay, and Sémillon.

Argentinean wineries are making a name for themselves on the world stage and a number of reliable producers ship to export markets. Look for Catena, Norton, Trapiche, Etchart, Finca Flichman, and Bodegas Lurton.

AUSTRALIA

Plans to be the third-largest wine exporter in the world by 2025. In the last five years, the amount under vine and the level of exports have almost doubled.

Australia's calling card is technology, innovation, and research. Much of this innovation has gone into increasing economies of scale – both in the vineyard and in the winery – and the result is litres and litres of clean, well-made wines at all price levels. Unless the rest of the world wakes up, it is going to be difficult to stop the tidal wave of wine that is headed our way.

1. Barossa Valley
2. Coonawarra
3. Clare Valley
4. Padthaway
5. Hunter Valley
6. Yarra Valley
7. Tasmania
8. Margaret River

In wine terms, Australia is a relatively small wine-producing nation – about an eighth of the output of Italy. But because of its geographic size, it can produce any style of wine imaginable, from cool climate steely whites to big, jammy warm climate reds.

Australia is in the process of developing an appellation system (Geographic Indications System) to identify the source of wines. The first level is *Produce of Australia*, followed by *South-Eastern Australia* (a catch-all designation for most export wines), then the five *States of Origin*. Each of these states is broken into *zones* and then *regions*.

Three grapes make up about half of the total plantings in Australia. Each has its own classic style:

- Shiraz – big, rich, spicy, jammy blackberry fruit
- Cabernet Sauvignon – intense, bright blackcurrant fruit
- Chardonnay – fat, full, toasty, ripe tropical fruit

You will also find Pinot Noir and Grenache for red wines and Sauvignon Blanc, Riesling, Semillon, and Verdelho – particularly from Western Australia – for the whites. Australian winemakers love to blend two grapes together and put both names on the label. It isn't uncommon to see Shiraz blended with Grenache (as in the Rhône) or Sauvignon Blanc with Semillon (as in Bordeaux).

Vintages are rarely an issue because the climate is so perfect most of the time. To be honest, the regions don't matter a whole lot either. It is the *producer* that is important in Australia. Here are some to look for: Tyrell's, Rosemount, Brokenwood, Chateau Tahbilk, Yarra Yering, Peter Lehmann, Penfolds, Wolf Blass, Wynns, Chateau Reynella, Yalumba, Lindemans, Hamilton, Chestnut Grove, and Cape Mentelle.

STICKIES

Australia's focus on fresh, dry table wines is fairly recent. Up to about 40 years ago, Aussie wines were usually sweet, port-like wines (a.k.a. "stickies") or came in a box. Now you can select fruity, well-made wines from many different grape varieties and at different price points.

South Australia

This is the largest wine-producing state and makes over half of all Australian wine. It includes some of the best wine regions including **Barossa Valley** for big Shiraz and Cabernet, **Coonawarra** for Cabernet, **Clare Valley** for Riesling, and **Padthaway** for Chardonnay and Sauvignon Blanc.

New South Wales

This state produces about a quarter of all Australian wine, a lot of which is high-production, low-grade wine, but there is good Shiraz to be found from the **Lower** and **Upper Hunter Valleys**. Semillon (no accent required) is a treat if you can find it.

Victoria

Although small, Victoria has the most wineries and individual styles of any state. In addition to being famous for sweet fortified Muscats (**Rutherglen**), some of the best Pinot Noir in Australia comes from the **Yarra Valley**.

Tasmania

The island of Tasmania is a cool climate region. It produces light Pinot Noirs and Chardonnay.

Western Australia

This state is known for its high-quality wines, especially those from **Margaret River**. Despite producing a scant 3% of Australia's wines, area winemakers receive more than their share of awards and recognition. Maybe it is the elegance and lightness of the wines that sets them apart from their burly kin to the east.

NEW ZEALAND

New Zealand may be a small country, in both geographic and wine-production terms, but it produces its share of quality wine, at least judging by the international acclaim showered on its wines, especially Sauvignon Blanc.

New Zealand is a cool climate region. The cooling winds of the Pacific Ocean and the mountains that form persistent rain clouds give New Zealand much cooler temperatures than one would think given its location. The climate varies between the two islands – the harvest in the north often precedes that of the south by six weeks.

Regulations are being developed to certify the origin of the grapes and the wine, and to delimit wine regions. Currently there are 14 regions; however, there are basically two distinct areas: the North Island and – wait for it – the South Island. In the warmer North Island, **Martinborough** (where some of the best Pinot Noir comes from),

Hawkes Bay, **Gisborne**, and **Wairarapa** are the key regions; in the South, it is **Marlborough** (New Zealand's most important region, famous for Sauvignon Blanc).

New Zealand wines are generally cleaner and leaner, with more balanced fruit and acidity, than their Aussie counterparts. The wine style has evolved to be better suited to food than most New World wine regions. Perhaps this explains the growing popularity of New Zealand wines around the world.

New Zealand is probably most famous for Sauvignon Blanc, especially the export Cloudy Bay. Chardonnay is still the most widely planted white wine grape, but now only by the slightest of margins. Gisborne is the place to look for good Chardonnay.

As for reds, Pinot Noir, New Zealand's third most planted grape, has made the most progress. Merlot also shows promise, as does Cabernet Sauvignon, especially in Hawkes Bay and Wairarapa, where each can ripen properly.

One company – Montana – dominates New Zealand wine production, with over 60% of the market. Other producers worth checking out include Villa Maria, Palliser Estate, Kim Crawford, Fairhall Downs, Ata Rangi (killer Pinot), C.J. Pask, Wairau River, Koura Bay, and Martinborough Vineyard.

SOUTH AFRICA

After years of isolation during apartheid, South Africa is re-emerging as an important wine region on the world stage. It ranks sixth in terms of production, with wines at all levels of quality, style, and price.

Until 1992, much of South Africa's wine industry was controlled by a large co-operative called KMV, which controlled prices but did little to improve the quality of the wine. Recent reforms changed this and now quality-minded estates are free to plant what they want, at yields that are more consistent with international standards. About 20 years ago, South Africa developed the Wines of Origin (WO) system to bring its wines in line with similar (European) appellation systems. It guarantees the origin of what's in the bottle. Only about one-third of South African wines fall under the WO, and more than half of total production is used for distillation.

Old Roots
In the New World, South Africa has the longest tradition for producing quality wine; the Dutch planted vines as early as 1654.

South Africa's vineyards are near Capetown, where the potentially high temperatures are tempered by cool ocean breezes. There are five wine regions, but it is the next level down in the WO system (the 12 or so districts) that is of interest to the consumer. The more notable ones are **Stellenbosch**, **Paarl**, **Robertson**, and **Overberg**. Other regions are gaining reputation as a flood of foreign investment enters the country.

> **Famous Sweetie**
> The historic district Constantia is famous for the legendary dessert wine by the same name. Constantia was considered at one time to be one of the greatest sweet wines in the world.

Steen (known elsewhere as Chenin Blanc) is the most-planted white wine grape and accounts for almost a fifth of total plantings. It's used to produce a variety of different styles from dry, everyday wines to late harvest sweeties. Chardonnay, and especially Sauvignon Blanc, are the wines to watch in the future.

Red varieties make up only about 15% of all plantings, and Cabernet Sauvignon is the most widely planted. It is often bottled in Bordeaux-style blends that have won recognition around the world. Cinsaut – which makes light and juicy red wines – used to be the leading red variety, but Cabernet Sauvignon is what everyone is betting on. Pinot Noir is showing great potential, especially in the district of Overberg. Syrah is also being planted and the results are promising.

South Africa may be better known for Pinotage (a crossing of Cinsaut and Pinot Noir) but it's actually only third in terms of red grape plantings. It makes an easy-drinking, earthy red wine that often has an unusual gaminess or burnt rubber smell.

While KMV (in Paarl) still exists, there are other new co-operatives including Winds of Change, Freedom Road, and New Beginnings. Other producers to look for include Kanonkop, Hamilton Russell, Bouchard Finlayson, Neil Ellis, Cape Point Vineyards, Thelema, Mulderbosch, and Meerlust.

THE ART OF TASTING WINE

OR LEARNING HOW TO SPIT

As of yet, we haven't had to teach anyone how to drink in our classes. That seems to come naturally – and very naturally to some. What we do instead is teach people how to taste.

Don't worry, you don't have to adopt some pretentious ritual just to be able to enjoy wine. Professional wine tasting is for professionals. But tasting like a pro opens up a whole new dimension to wine that you might not even know exists.

Tasting anything is a multi-sensory experience, whether it's a plate of chips or a glass of wine. While you think you're using only your mouth to taste, your other senses actually play a bigger role. Just try to taste those chips with a cold.

When you taste wine you use your senses in order: sight, smell, touch, and taste. We'll leave out hearing because we have yet to meet anyone capable of differentiating between the sound of an '89 Bordeaux sloshing around in a glass and a cup of coffee.

Wine tasting is easy to learn and a bit like cooking. At first you're stumbling around in the kitchen, then before you know it you're making spaghetti bolognese. And in no time at all you're inviting everyone over for dinner.

With a little practice, and some patience, you too will be tasting like a pro and inviting your friends to wine parties.

THE "EYES" HAVE IT

Just as we expect milk to be white and opaque, we should expect our wine to look a certain way. Even before we pour the wine, visual clues on the bottle and the label tell us a lot about the wine inside: where it's from, what grape or grapes it's made from, how old it is. Even the cork – once it's out of the bottle – can give clues as to the age and providence of the wine. If it's a relatively young wine, there won't be much to look at: the part of the cork that touched the wine is probably wet but not much else. Older corks, however, will be much darker. If the cork is in bad shape, the wine may not have been stored properly.

And what about the wine itself? Why do pros stare at their wines for so long? Essentially, they are looking at three things: clarity, colour, and intensity.

> **Crystals**
> You may find sugar-like tartrate crystals sticking to the bottom of the wine cork or as part of the sediment at the bottom of the bottle. The latter is quite common in certain older German wines. Tartrates are harmless and indicate the wine has been stored in cold conditions. Many winemakers now cold-stabilize their wines before bottling to eliminate these crystals.

Clarity

Is the wine bright and clear or dull and hazy? At one time this was very important but nowadays we don't see as many badly made, hazy wines. Brightness, on the other hand, is important, as it's a sign of high acidity and of high quality.

If the wine is a sparkling wine, then obviously you should expect to see bubbles. Some still wines (Vinho Verde, for example) may have a slight spritz, but otherwise bubbles, where there aren't supposed to be any, aren't a good sign.

And there shouldn't be anything floating in your wine or sitting on the bottom of the glass. Chunky bits are okay for orange juice but not wine.

Colour

Certain wines have certain colours. You can use any term you want to describe the colour of a wine – and some people do – but here are a few colours, or more precisely *hues*, you should expect to see in wine:

White Wines	Red Wines	Rosé Wines
Green	Purple	Blue pink
Lemon	Ruby	Orange pink
Straw	Cherry	Salmon
Gold	Garnet	
Amber	Brick	
	Mahogany	

In addition to helping you describe the wine, here's what else the colour suggests:

- **Age** – White wines gain colour as they age (from greenish tints to amber), while red wines lose colour (from purple hues to mahogany). As they age, wines oxidize, just like an apple core left on the worktop overnight. A very young Chardonnay, for example, shouldn't be amber. If it is, it could mean there's something wrong with the wine.
- **The grape type** – Fuller-bodied wines are deeper coloured. Cabernet Sauvignon generally produces a darker-coloured wine than Pinot Noir, and certain grape varieties (e.g., Grenache or Nebbiolo) brown more rapidly than other varieties.
- **Origin** – Cool climate regions produce lighter-coloured wines and warm climate regions produce deeper-coloured wines.

> *Where Does the Colour Go?*
> In addition to oxidizing as they age, red wines polymerize – a word used to describe how colour molecules link together over time to form larger molecules. Eventually they get too heavy to stay soluble and fall to the bottom of the bottle as sediment. If you open a 20-year-old port, for example, you will see the sediment that has formed on the side of the bottle (if the bottle was stored on its side). The first to go are the purple molecules (anthocyanins), leaving the more reddish-orange tannins behind. Knowing how and when these changes occur is a professional taster's "party trick."

- **Winemaking technique** – Overripe grapes, longer skin contact during fermentation, and oak ageing all result in more deeply coloured wines.

Intensity

Depth refers to the intensity of the colour. In the glass, this isn't uniform: the deepest colour is usually at the centre of the glass, getting paler towards the rim. Here are a few key words, and the order in which they would be used, to describe depth:

Watery – > Pale – > Medium – > Deep – > Opaque.

For example, a young German Riesling wine will have a watery intensity, while a young Shiraz will look opaque. As the Shiraz ages it will start to lighten at the rim first (where the wine meets the edge of the glass).

TASTE – IT'S ALL IN YOUR NOSE!

For the enjoyment of wine, your nose – your sense of smell – is the most important tool you have. When you *taste* a wine, you actually *smell* it. Your tongue is capable of differentiating only four tastes – sweet, sour, bitter, and salty – while your nose is sensitive to over 10,000! Since there are 200 or so known odorous compounds in wine, it's no contest – the nose wins.

We will not go into detail about how the nose works, but essentially what goes up your nose when you inhale are molecules in a gaseous state. Everything, except maybe rocks, gives off these gaseous molecules. The molecules are trapped in your nasal cavity, in the mucous layer, and the odours are transferred through impulses to the olfactory bulb and eventually to the brain. Here it triggers your memory of the smell and tells you, "Ah, strawberries!" However, if you don't have a memory of that smell, you won't be able to put a name to it.

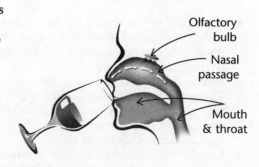

Olfactory bulb

Nasal passage

Mouth & throat

Wines Have Noses, Too
You will hear people refer to the "nose" of a wine. This refers to the
"smell." Instead of saying your wine "smells" of strawberries, you say, "I
detect strawberries on the nose." If a wine has a "big nose," it means the
smell is intense.

Practice, Practice, Practice

Professional tasters have very good smell memories. For some, it's a gift,
but for most it's learned. Becoming more aware of how things around
you smell can strengthen your memory. Women are thought to have
better senses of smell and in our experience this is true.

People who smell certain things on a regular basis (florists for
example) find the intensity of familiar smells diminished when they
encounter them elsewhere. This is called *adaptation* and also happens
with wine.

We will show you how to actually smell a wine later; first, let's talk
about what to look for when *describing* the smell of a wine.

Aroma

Let's get this straight at the outset: there are no strawberries, or any other
fruit (other than grapes), in wine. It just may smell like strawberries.
Wine odours come from three sources: the grape, fermentation, and
ageing.

Aroma refers to odours associated with the grapes. Aroma is more
obvious in young wines and pungent-smelling wines like Sauvignon
Blanc or Muscat. Pros call it the *primary aroma*.

It's fairly easy to describe wine aroma. Wine people use common
items – plants, fruits, and flowers especially – partly because they belong
to similar chemical groups (that's why things smell similar), but mainly
because they provide a common vocabulary. Here are some examples of
wine aromas:

Aroma		Grape
Fruity	Citrus	Riesling
	Black fruits (e.g., blackcurrants)	Cabernet Sauvignon
	Red fruits (e.g., raspberries)	Pinot Noir
Floral	Violets	Nebbiolo
	Roses	Gewürztraminer
	Orange blossom	Muscat
Vegetal/Herbal	Asparagus or cut grass	Sauvignon Blanc
	Green pepper	Cabernet Franc
Spicy/Nutty	Black pepper	Syrah/Shiraz
	Almonds	Garganega

Bouquet

Bouquet not only sounds more sophisticated than aroma but also describes more sophisticated and complex odours. These are the odours associated with fermentation and ageing. They add a layer of complexity that leads directly to our overall enjoyment and appreciation of wine.

During fermentation, yeasts and bacteria act to create a new set of odours. Certain yeasts create their own aromatics, some good and some bad. (Wild yeasts can induce some less desirable odours.) Wooden barrels, if used, make their own individual contribution to the wine's bouquet. All of these transcend the wine's primary aromas and create a whole new odour profile. Barrel-fermented Chardonnay, for example, smells quite different from Chardonnay made in stainless steel tanks.

In wines that have been aged – in barrels and/or bottles – a different set of changes occurs. In barrels the wine oxidizes and certain components of the wood (oak, for example) are dissolved in the wine. This is the origin of the smell of vanilla in oak-aged wines. Newer barrels contribute more to the bouquet than older barrels. In the bottle, the wine has very little contact with oxygen, so the process is more or less *reductive*. Harsher odours slowly become muted and more harmonized.

Some wines take longer than others to develop their bouquet; however, for most of the wines on the market the winery has made this decision for you. They are ready to drink when you buy them. For the others, check vintage charts or ask for advice.

Follow Your Nose

What else might your nose lead you to? Here are a few clues:

- **Cleanliness** – Wine should be free of unpleasant odours. You wouldn't drink a glass of milk that had soured, would you?
- **Grape variety** – Noble varieties (e.g., Cabernet Sauvignon and Riesling) are more distinctive.
- **Grape quality** – Poorer quality grapes are usually overly intense (e.g., North American labrusca grapes) or "foxy." And overcropping any vine produces grapes of weaker character or less intensity.
- **Age** – Recently bottled wines often suffer from something called "bottle fatigue": the wine is "dumb" and you can't really smell anything. Older wines can be "closed" at first, and need some time to open up. A few minutes in a decanter can speed this process along.

IS IT OK TO TOUCH?

The touch factor in wine refers to its *texture*, sometimes called mouthfeel. When you slosh the wine around in your mouth, it feels a certain way. Some wines are smoother (e.g., Pinot Noir), some are harsher (e.g., a young Cabernet Sauvignon), and some are mouth filling (e.g., a California Chardonnay). What's going on and what does it mean?

- *Astringency* is the puckering or drying sensation you feel on your gums. Astringency comes from tannins, either from the grape itself or from the barrels in which the wine was aged. Try a mouthful of very strong tea and you'll get the idea of what astringency feels like. High acidity in a wine will accentuate the sensation of astringency. Astringency is often confused with bitterness, but they are two separate things. One is a feeling and the other is a taste.
- *Body* is a more difficult term to define. It's the feeling of weight and richness in your mouth as a result of alcohol, sugars, and intensity of flavour. Think about it in terms of fabrics (silk, velvet, wool) or viscosity (watery, thin, full, or thick).
- High levels of *alcohol* will produce a hot sensation down the centre of your tongue and can be perceived as both a sweet and a bitter sensation. That is why some dry red wines like Amarone, with high alcohol levels, are thought to be sweet. Alcohol also coats the surface of your mouth and distributes flavours around your palate.

Let's not forget bubbles – that "prickle" on the tip of your tongue that comes from sparkling wine. When they are supposed to be there, bubbles in wine give us joy. But the carbon dioxide in these wines actually creates a mild pain sensation in our brains, putting our taste buds into overdrive and intensifying flavours.

Finally, the serving temperature of the wine can have an impact on the perception of astringency, body, and alcohol. Cool serving temperatures will de-emphasize a wine's texture; too warm, and the alcohol in particular will be overemphasized.

Measuring Your Mouth

The texture of a wine in your mouth can suggest the following:

- **Grape variety** – Red wines, especially young red wines, have more tannin. Certain grape varieties (e.g., Nebbiolo) are more tannic than others (e.g., Merlot), while some varieties (e.g., Muscadet) feel lighter bodied.
- **Origin of the wine** – A wine from a warm climate region will feel fuller bodied than one from a cool climate region, and the sensation caused by higher alcohol levels will be stronger.
- **Fermentation technique** – If the wine has been fermented in oak for a period of time, you will detect tannins or astringency from the oak. Oak tannins are softer than grape tannins, and are more apparent on the sides and back of your mouth (as opposed to grape tannins, which are apparent on your teeth and gums).

STICK OUT YOUR TONGUE

Different parts of your tongue are more sensitive to certain tastes than other parts. That's why the pros slosh the wine around in their mouths. When you taste something sweet, for example, you should pick it up on the tip of your tongue. You'll taste sweet elsewhere, but the tip is the most sensitive. Sweetness, then, should be the first thing you notice in a wine.

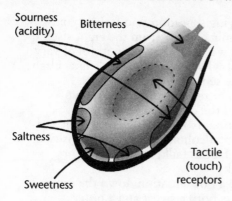

Sourness (acidity)

Bitterness

Saltness

Sweetness

Tactile (touch) receptors

Acidity (tartness) is sensed at the sides of the tongue and will probably make your mouth water, just as it does when you drink fresh-squeezed orange juice. Acidity gives wines their "zing."

Bitterness – like the taste of tonic water or strong black coffee – is mainly sensed at the back of the tongue. This explains why some people comment on the "bitterness" of a wine once they've swallowed it – it is the last thing they taste. A touch of bitterness is considered to be an attribute in young red wines, and in particular some Italian red wines.

Speaking of Tongues

Once the wine is in your mouth, what will your tongue tell you?

- **Balance** – Acidity should offset sweetness, otherwise the wine will be cloying. Any one component in excess will make the wine taste unpleasant.
- **Grape variety** – Certain grapes (e.g., Sauvignon Blanc and Barbera) have more acidity than others.
- **Origin of the wine** – Grapes grown in cool climate regions generally have more acidity. Italian wines tend to have a touch of bitterness on the finish.
- **Fermentation technique** – Some winemakers prefer to leave a little residual sugar in their wines, some a lot, making the wines off dry, sweet, or luscious.

WHO GETS THE LAST WORD?

Remember, all you can discern at this time is sweet, sour, and bitter. You don't *taste* strawberries in wine, you smell them. Now, if you swallow the wine, you might actually think you taste strawberries. That's because there is a secondary route to the olfactory bulb at the back of your throat called the *retronasal passage*.

As you breathe out after swallowing, wine odours are volatized by the warmth of your mouth and pushed out over that mucous layer again. So when you think you are *tasting* strawberries, you are actually *smelling* them again. Your nose always has to have the last word.

Umami

Savoury foods (shellfish, meats, and cheeses) are said to be high in umami and may increase the sensation of bitterness in a wine. Umami is considered to be the fifth taste.

PUTTING IT ALL TOGETHER

When it comes to tasting wine, you have to pull all of your senses together. When you do you can start to make decisions or even assessments about the wine. Do you like it? Should you drink it? Should you give it to your sister for her birthday? Is it good value and should you buy more?

Here are three things to consider as you combine your senses:

- *Finish* is the lingering impression a wine leaves long after you have swallowed it. If the wine has a "short" finish (a few seconds) the flavour disappears quickly. Ten seconds is considered medium and fifteen seconds long. Too long and the wine has overstayed its welcome. If the wine was inexpensive and had a long finish, buy more!
- *Balance* describes the harmony between acidity, sugar, alcohol, tannins, flavour, aroma, and bouquet. This isn't the exclusive domain of superior wines; even humble table wines can exhibit balance. It's the best indicator of good winemaking.
- *Quality*, of course, is subjective. What really matters is what *you* think of the wine. It isn't about price, expert reviews, or even what your friends say. If you like the wine, then just say so.

GETTING READY TO SPIT

Now we get to the good part. Wine tasting requires a little preparation, so here are a few things to do before getting started.

Put yourself in the right frame of mind. If you just spent two hours battling rush hour traffic, maybe this isn't a good time to taste wine. Your senses are most acute in the morning, say around 10 AM – or mid-afternoon, before you have dinner. Tasting when starving or after a full meal isn't a good idea, either – especially after a double anchovy and garlic pizza! Even tasting wine after drinking a coffee will have an effect on how the wine smells and tastes. If you are tasting for fun – say as part of a get-together with friends – then you'll probably be doing it in the evening. In this case just avoid strongly flavoured foods.

Avoid cologne or perfume, too. It will have an effect on what you smell. And don't brush your teeth just before you taste. If you do, all the wines will taste minty.

Make sure the lighting is good. Remember, you have to see the wine. Save the dim lights for the romantic dinner afterwards.

Create space. A nice big table is better than a small corner of your kitchen – especially if this is a social affair. If possible, use a white surface. A tablecloth would be great but you may not like the inevitable red wine spills. A sheet of white paper works fine – anything that you can put the wine against to see its true colour.

Blind Tasting
In a blind taste you are given a sample (or more) of wine and asked to evaluate it without knowing where it was made or what grapes were used. That way price, the producer, or any other factor does not influence your assessment of the wine. It's also a fun party game.

Wine tasting checklist:

- Make sure the wines are at the right temperature (about 50°F/10°C for white wines and 60°F/16°C for reds). You'll get about 12 samples from each bottle.
- Unless the bottles have screw tops, don't forget the corkscrew.
- Clean, clear glasses – preferably all the same size and shape if you're tasting more than one wine or have friends over. Make sure the glasses have stems and hold about 25cl (8-9 ounces). (See page 99 for more information on glasses.)
- Have something to take notes with when you taste. That way you have a record of what you thought about the wine. It will come in handy when you taste a whole series of wines and want to remember something about them later.
- If you're tasting lots of wines, you might want to have plain bread, breadsticks, and room-temperature mineral water (not the fizzy kind) handy to cleanse your palate. If it's one or two wines, don't bother. But avoid the Gorgonzola or anchovies until after you've finished tasting the wine.
- You'll need something to spit in if you aren't planning on swallowing, preferably something opaque because no one likes to look at someone else's spit. It also needs to be large enough so you don't have to worry about being overly accurate. The pros use spittoons but a paper cup works just fine.

GETTING THE WINE OUT

Now comes the fun part: opening the bottle. This is where you can demonstrate how co-ordinated you are. Like shuffling a deck of cards, with practice, you too can look impressive opening a bottle.

What's between You and the Wine

Well, usually just the traditional cork. But nowadays there are many different closures being used. You might find plastic corks (hard to get out), screw caps, and even crown caps (like beer bottles).

Corks, made from the bark of cork trees in Spain and Portugal, are still the most popular means of sealing bottles of wine. Over 90% of wines sold in bottles use a natural cork. Corks hold the wine inside, yet allow a minute amount of oxygen to enter the bottle. For quality wines, this is said to help the wine's development.

What about the other closures – do they work? In some cases, they work quite well, but the jury is out on whether these will eventually

---

Cork Taint
Corks are usually bleached prior to washing. Occasionally the chlorine reacts with moulds in the cork and can produce off-odours in the wine.
    If you detect an eau-de-musty basement smell in the wine, it is "corked" and you shouldn't drink it.

replace corks. We're starting to see more high-end wineries, mostly New World ones, converting to one of these options. They are just not willing to compromise on quality by subjecting the wine to an unpredictable little chunk of bark.

We suspect natural corks are going to be around for a long time yet. Wine is a tradition-bound industry, and purists still like to believe in the mysterious transference of oxygen through the cork. And having the sommelier flick off the cap of your wine bottle with a beer opener just isn't the same as the elegant performance of removing the cork.

Where's the Cork?

Actually, the first thing that's between you and the wine is the *capsule* or covering over the top of the bottle neck. Capsules used to be made of lead; now they're made of plastic or aluminum.

First, cut off the capsule below the second lip of the bottle. Most corkscrews have a little knife or cutting edge to help you do this. Next, check out the top of the cork. If it's an older wine, there might be crud on top of the cork. This is okay because it indicates the wine has been stored in a humid place – a good sign. Don't worry, the crud won't have gone into the wine, and to make sure it doesn't, just wipe it off with a damp cloth.

The Pointy End Goes in First

It's hard to believe that a piece of cork can cause so much trouble. We've had to open wines with corks wedged in so tightly that the force of yanking the cork out pulled some wine out with it. And we've opened wines with corks that have compressed so much over the years that they have slipped down the neck of the bottle and into the wine below.

How you get the screw part of the corkscrew into the cork will depend on the design of the corkscrew you use. There are three that we recommend. They all cost under £10 and do the job nicely.

- **Waiter's corkscrew** – Most people in the restaurant business use this compact corkscrew. Tucked into its handle is a small knife that folds out for cutting the capsule foil.

  Waiter's corkscrew

  To use one, make sure the bottle is on a solid surface. (Experienced servers can open a bottle in the air but they've had lots of practice.) And make sure you've removed the foil or plastic capsule first. If there is a little plastic tab on top of the cork, just prepare to drill through it.

  Next, gently press the point of the spiral (called the *worm*) into the centre of the cork, holding the corkscrew at a 45-degree angle. As you begin twisting the worm into the cork, straighten it up so it goes in vertically. Twist it in a clockwise direction about four or five turns, until it is almost completely in the cork. Hook the metal piece onto the lip of the bottle. Hold it on the lip while you pull up the handle and the worm, drawing out the cork.

Probably the best way to learn how to use one is to watch your waiter the next time you are in a restaurant. If your birthday is coming up, ask for a waiter's corkscrew that has a Teflon® worm – you won't believe the difference it makes.

- **Screwpull corkscrew** – This excellent version for home is simple and fast to use. It has a longer Teflon®-coated worm that works on almost every cork. Some models come with a foil cutter, but it isn't as easy to use as the one on the waiter's corkscrew. Screwpull sells an extra accessory designed for this purpose.

Screwpull

    Once the cork is exposed, place the Screwpull on top of the bottle with a plastic leg resting on each side of the neck. The point of the worm should be sitting on top of the cork. Hold the legs against the top of the bottle and begin twisting the handle clockwise, driving the worm into the cork. Keep twisting, and the cork slides right out of the bottle neck. No pulling required.

    The Screwpull works only for standard 75cl bottles. Larger format bottles have too large a neck for the device.

- **Butler's Friend** – For older bottles with fragile corks we recommend a corkscrew called the Butler's Friend or the Ah-So. This unique corkscrew gets the cork out without piercing a hole in it. It requires technique and a lot of practice, but once you get the knack, you'll love using it.

    Holding the handle, slide the longer prong between the cork and the bottle top, gently working it down. Then insert the other prong against the cork on the other side. Rock the prongs back and forth, with a gentle downward

Butler's Friend or Ah-So

push, until the handle is close to the top of the bottle. Twist and pull up the opener until the cork is freed. If the cork is loose, however, it may just push the cork down the neck and into the wine – that's where patience comes in.

Everyone breaks the cork now and then – don't worry about it. Just reinsert the corkscrew at an extreme angle, and ease the cork out. If that doesn't work, poke it into the bottle. A little bit of cork in the diet never hurt anyone. Just don't serve your guests first. If it's really bad, pour the wine through a coffee filter.

How to Not Drink the Gunk at the Bottom of the Bottle

If you have just opened a bottle of older red wine, there is a good chance that it will have some sediment on the bottom of the bottle. You don't really want that in your glass. It won't kill you but it will make the wine hazier and less brilliant. To keep this from happening, you – or your waiter – will have to *decant* the wine.

There are three reasons for decanting a wine:

- To separate the wine from the naturally forming sediment or deposit. This is more common in older, full-bodied, tannic red wines and in vintage ports. There shouldn't be sediment in a white wine;
- To aerate, or help a wine breathe or open up; and
- For show!

At home, you don't need a special decanter for this – any clear glass or crystal jug will work provided that it's large enough to hold the contents of a bottle and has a large surface area to expose the wine to air. We use a glass jug as a decanter. It looks great, works well, and is easy to clean.

If you are decanting for aeration, just open and empty the wine vigorously into the decanter. Do this about half an hour before the meal and enjoy.

Decanting for sediment is a little trickier:

- First, make sure the bottle has been upright for a few hours to let the sediment settle down to the bottom of the bottle. If the wine has been stored for a number of years (vintage port, for example) you may want to keep it upright for a day or so.
- Open the wine as you normally would but take extra care not to shake the bottle. With a light source behind the bottle, and the decanter in your other hand hold the wine label-side up in one hand. *Slowly* pour the contents of the wine into the decanter.
- Continue pouring until you see the dark sediment pass into the neck of the bottle. Stop decanting and start enjoying the wine. We usually don't recommend drinking the ounce or so left in the bottle.

Does Wine Breathe?

Aeration, or letting a wine breathe, gives it contact with air to improve the aromas and taste of the wine. This is for full-bodied, higher alcohol, tannic young red wines that need time to be at their best – Bordeaux, Syrah, and Barolo for example. Older white wines (Burgundy, for example) also seem to benefit from a little aeration.

If wines didn't get the time they needed in the bottle, you can help them along by getting oxygen into the wine as quickly as possible. Give the wine in your glass a few good swirls, or decant it as we just described. There are some who insist that the aromas and flavours of a wine are lost by decanting it, and they prefer to aerate the wine by simply swirling it in their glass.

You can go too far with this breathing thing, however. Wines left too long exposed to air can become flat and dull, or worse, oxidized. Oxygen improves the wine to a point, but then causes it to decline steadily into something un-tasty.

I'm not coming out 'til I'm good and ready!

HOW TO OPEN A BOTTLE OF SPARKLING WINE WITHOUT KILLING YOUR GUESTS

Opening a bottle of sparkling wine is quite different and much more risky. Despite what you see at the Formula One winner's circle and in films, sparkling wines aren't supposed to be opened with a loud pop and a gush of foam. And as funny as it may seem in a film, the cork can be a dangerous little projectile. Some of the unique things about a champagne bottle – the wire cage over the cork and the thicker glass – were designed to protect you and your guests from harm.

Opening a bottle of sparkling wine is easy if you maintain control of the bottle and let the escaping pressure do all the work. Here's how you can open a bottle without putting your guests or your pets at risk:

- *Never use a corkscrew.*
- Make sure the wine is well chilled (under 50°F/10°C). This will suppress some of the pressure that can cause it to open explosively. If the bottle has been in an ice bucket, dry it off.
- Tear off the foil to reveal the wire cage that wraps over the cork. Press one of your thumbs over the cork and hold it there while you undo the cage with your other hand. This can be tricky so point the wine away from your loved ones, the china, and that big window in the front room.
- Grasp the cork tightly while holding the bottom of the bottle firmly with your other hand. Hold the bottle at a 45° angle and gently start turning the bottle away from you while holding the cork steady. The pressure in the bottle will slowly begin to push the cork out. Control the pressure while slowly easing out the cork. It's okay to stop for a few seconds to prevent any foaming incidents. Have the glasses ready just in case.

Ready to Punt
One extra-special bonus with champagne and many other sparkling wines is the chance to pour using the punt, that indentation at the bottom of the bottle. This really impresses people. Just put your thumb into the punt and rest the underside of the bottle against your palm and fingers as you pour.

DO YOU NEED GLASSES?

Why spend money on glasses; why not just spend it on more or better wine? Better glasses improve the look, the smell, the taste, and the feel of the wine. Sadly, they won't turn a £10 wine into a £20 wine. But if they improve the tasting experience, though, perhaps that's all that matters.

Do you have to spend a lot to get good glassware? You can if you want. Riedel, a brand of Austrian crystal glassware, makes wine glasses for every grape type and wine style imaginable, but they aren't cheap.

To start off, you might be happier with an all-purpose, and inexpensive, glass that will still make a difference to the appearance, aroma, and taste of the wine you drink. If you are thinking of buying a set of these glasses, here's what to look for and what to avoid:

	Go For:	Avoid:
Colour	Clear	Tinted or cut glass
Weight	Light, with thin rim	Heavy, with bead on rim
Size	10–12 oz (280–340 ml)	Goldfish bowls
Shape	Tulip	Parallel sides, like a hi-ball glass
Other	A stem	Logos

- Clear glass allows you to see the colour of the wine, without it being distorted by the appearance of the glass itself.
- A lighter-weight glass lets you concentrate on the feel of the wine in your mouth, not the feel of the glass.
- A larger size gives you the room you need to swirl your wine without having it slosh over the sides.
- The shape, tapered in toward the rim, concentrates the aromas and enhances the taste experience. You might want to buy a different set of glasses for sparkling wine – tall flutes and not those saucer-type glasses from the sixties – as they concentrate the bubbles more in the glass.
- The stem lets you hold the glass without getting fingerprints on the bowl, or warming up the wine.

Follow these rules and you can increase your wine-drinking pleasure.

Filling the Glass

We used to be disappointed when we were served glasses of wine that weren't filled right to the rim. Now we know better.

When serving wine with a meal, glasses should be filled to the widest part of the glass bowl, about 110–140 ml (4 or 5 oz) per glassful. This allows for more aeration, allowing the wine to open up and release its aromas into the air. It also gives you enough room to swirl the wine, again to release those aromas into the bowl of the glass so that you can enjoy them. If you are tasting wine, and not serving it with a meal, a couple of ounces is sufficient.

When pouring sparkling wine, you should use a succession of small pours so the wine doesn't foam up and pour over the rim.

TASTING LIKE A PRO

Now that you've successfully opened the wine, you're ready to taste it. While the pros have their rituals, all you need is a system that helps build the case for or against the wine, yet doesn't require a lot of time. With practice you can perform our Four-Step Programme, in a matter of seconds. Of course, if you become a world-class taster, or you really enjoy the wine, you'll want to spend more time with each wine before you drink it down.

The 4 S's

Here's our *Four-Step Programme for Enjoyable Wine Tasting*.

1. See
2. Sniff
3. Sip
4. Spit (or swallow)

Don't worry about the process; it is more important to think about the wine and how it appeals to you. To best experience the wine, pour about 1 or 2 oz (30–60 ml) into your glass. That way you will have adequate room to swirl the wine in the bowl without spilling. You might not think this will be enough wine, but trust us, you will get four to six good sips out of it. Besides, it leaves even more to drink later if you like the wine.

See
Although most wines are pretty clean nowadays, a visual inspection of the wine is still an important part of the process. Here's what the pros do and what they're looking for:

- Looking down at your glass, check for clarity – is the wine bright and clear? Are there any bits of cork? Bubbles?
- Tilt the glass at about a 45-degree angle over whatever white surface you're using. You are now looking at the colour (hue) and intensity of the wine. Look at the core or centre of the wine first, not where it meets the glass (the rim).
- Use simple words to describe what you see. For example, "pale, greenish yellow" or "deep, ruby red" are good descriptors.
- Now look at the rim. If the colour extends all the way to the rim, this suggests a younger wine. If the rim edge is pale or watery, it's probably a more mature wine. The wider the rim, the more mature the wine.

Nice Legs

The streams that run down the side of your glass after you swirl it are called "tears" or "legs." This indicates that evaporation rate of the alcohol in the wine, the surface tension, and other technical things. Wines with more alcohol appear to have more "legs." You can't really draw too many conclusions about the wine from the legs, but they are nice to look at.

Sniff
Here's where you get to *swirl* the wine like you've seen the pros do. But before you do, let it settle for a few seconds. Swirling the wine can mask some faults.

- Once it has settled, lift the glass to your nose and take a quick sniff. What do you smell? Is the wine clean? Is what you smell weak or pronounced?
- To swirl, hold the stem or base of the glass and make a few small counter-clockwise circles. At first, do this with your glass on the table. When you get good at it, you can do it in the air like the pros. Now you know why we said to buy large glasses. Swirling takes practice so give yourself lots of space early on and don't wear anything white.

- Swirl the glass a few times, then get your nose right into the glass and take a deep but short sniff. What's the first thing that comes to mind? A fruit? A vegetable? Your Grandmother's baking? Take a couple of more sniffs to see what else you detect. Write down whatever comes to mind.

Remember, smell is personal – whatever is triggered in your brain is yours and no one can tell you you're wrong. What's great about wine tasting is that you are always right; if you think you smell roses, you smell roses! Of course, certain smells are associated with certain grapes from certain regions. In a red wine it is unlikely that you are getting a citrus smell and white wines don't smell like raspberries. And you shouldn't smell turkey in *any* wine.

Three or four sniffs is enough. Any more and you will tire out your nose or look pretentious. Even if you came up with only a few words, don't worry – smelling takes practice.

Sip

Now you are ready to try the wine. You are looking for "touch" and "taste" sensations.

- Take a sip – about a good tablespoonful – and swish or slosh it around in your mouth. Don't swallow (or spit) yet. Try to hold it in your mouth for a few seconds to get the full effect.

   What level of sweetness (on the tip of your tongue) or bitterness (on the back of your tongue) do you detect? How about a tingle on the sides of your tongue? Does it make your mouth pucker or water? Is the wine silky or coarse, light bodied or full? Are there any bubbles? Does the wine feel balanced – in the way a juicy peach has aroma, flavour, sweetness, and acidity? Is the wine alcoholic (a burning sensation on your tongue)?

   Look for indications of anything out of balance. Write down whatever comes to mind. Does your taste suggest anything different from what you smelled? Or does it confirm what you smelled?

Keep in mind certain wines are supposed to have certain characteristics – Sauvignon Blanc should be dry and crisp and Cabernet Sauvignon should feel full and more alcoholic.

To spit or swallow?

If you are planning on tasting several wines and you have a spittoon handy, it's a good idea to spit rather than swallow. You start to lose your objectivity after four or five samples.

- Try another taste. This time let the wine rest on top of your tongue and gently inhale over the top of it without swallowing – sort of like a reverse whistle. By drawing air into your mouth you are intensifying the volatile odours in the wine. This can be tricky at first so wear dark clothes and keep a napkin handy.
- Now swallow or spit, but this time exhale through your nose. What do you smell now? Is it different from what you first smelled in the wine? More or less intense? Are there any new aromas?

Now it's time to draw some conclusions about the wine. Did you like it? Don't be afraid to talk about the wine. A few well-chosen words can help place the wine in your memory bank.

Reputable magazines and wine writers often use numerical systems to rate wines, but don't get blinded by 100-point systems or five-star evaluations. Just remember that the only way to evaluate a wine properly is to taste it yourself.

Using Your Words

Most people haven't developed a wine vocabulary. They can describe what an apple pie smells like when it is baking or the smell of sports equipment left in its bag from last season but they can't easily describe a wine. We assume you're in the same boat, so here are some words to start thinking about and to use when you want to describe what you're tasting.

You might think some of the "smell words" should be in the "bad words" column. However, you can use *herbaceous* or *vegetal* to describe Sauvignon Blanc because its smell is usually associated with asparagus or cut grass. And that's okay in the context of a Sauvignon Blanc, but not a Chardonnay, which doesn't usually have vegetal characteristics. Older red Burgundies can also smell vegetal, like "rotting leaves." It is all in how you interpret the smell.

Sight Words	Smell Words	Texture Words	Bad Words
• Bright	• Buttery	• Astringent	• Acetone
• Bubbles	• Clean	• Chalky	• Ammonia
• Clear	• Earthy	• Chewy	• Buttery
• Cloudy	• Floral	• Creamy	(strong)
• Deep	• Fruity	• Crisp	• Cheesy
• Dull	• Gamey	• Delicate	• Corked
• Hazy	• Grapey	• Dry	• Garlic
• Intense	• Herbaceous	• Fine	• Geranium
• Legs	• Jammy	• Firm	• Horsey
• Opaque	• Juicy	• Flabby	• Leesy
• Pale	• Minerals	• Harsh	• Mouldy
	• Nutty	• Heavy	• Mousey
	• Perfumed	• Hot	• Plastic
	• Pronounced	• Lean	• Putrid
	• Ripe	• Light	• Rotten eggs
	• Rustic	• Luscious	• Rubbery
	• Spicy	• Prickly	• Sauerkraut
	• Subtle	• Racy	• Sherry
	• Tired	• Rich	• Soapy
	• Vegetal	• Robust	• Sour
	• Weak	• Silky	• Sulphur
	• Yeasty	• Smooth	• Vinegar
	• Youthful	• Soft	• Wet cardboard
		• Tannic	
		• Thin	

But how many words do I have to remember?
People ask us this question all the
time. They don't want to say
something wrong and the list can be
intimidating. If you keep your nose
alert to smells around you, you
really don't need to memorize a list
at all. You're just building your
memory.

That said, certain fruit words are
called upon more frequently than
others, so here they are on the right:

White Wines	Red Wines
• Apples	• Blackberries
• Apricots	• Blackcurrants
• Lemons	• Cherries
• Limes	• Plums
• Melons	• Prunes
• Peaches	• Raisins
• Pineapple	• Raspberries
• Tropical fruits	• Strawberries

The "bad words" – When good wines go bad
It happens, good wines go bad. Sometimes they were made that way and
sometimes something happened on the way to the wine shop or on the
shop shelf. If you didn't store it properly, the wine could even have gone
bad while it was under your care. That's learning the hard way!

The drawback to learning how to taste properly is that it brings out all
the good *and* the bad characteristics in the wine. Poorly made or
defective wines aren't up to the challenge. While you'll learn to
distinguish between something unfamiliar and something defective, you
may also be able to uncover some flaws in good wines.

Lychees?
**We purposely didn't put lychee on the fruit word list because it only
comes into play with one wine: Gewürztraminer. Many people, however,
are unfamiliar with its smell. If you want to try lychee fruit, buy a tin of
them. It's the closest to what you smell in the wine.**

Flaws or defects make a wine undrinkable or diminish the overall
experience of drinking the wine. For example, wine shouldn't remind you
of vinegar, a musty cellar, rotten eggs, or sherry (unless it is sherry, of
course). Unusual aromas in wine are usually a result of bad winemaking
practices, contamination, or poor storage. Either something was in the
wine before it was bottled, something was in the bottle or on the cork
that wasn't supposed to be there, or something affected the wine because
of the way it was stored. To be fair, cork taint isn't necessarily a result of
bad winemaking; some corks may have been faulty when the winemaker
bought them.

Even before you put the wine to your nose to sniff, take note of what
it looks like. If you notice a haze, prematurely browning colours, or
bubbles when there shouldn't be any, pay special attention to the wine
when you do sniff it. The following substances occasionally appear in the
wine and may affect its appearance. However, they're essentially harmless:

- **Sediment** – These are the solids that precipitate out of tannic red wines
as they age. Pour carefully or decant so you don't drink any.
- **Tartrates** – These are more common in white wines. Found on the base
of the cork or settled at the bottom of the bottle, tartrates look like glass
crystals but aren't. Pour carefully and they won't get in your glass.

- **Cork pieces** – These little bits of cork, left from incomplete cork removal, won't hurt you – just have fun fishing them out of your glass.

Even if you are unfamiliar with the grape type or the wine itself, the wine should smell like wine, and it should always smell "clean." Very rarely – in probably less than 5% of the bottles you drink – you may find an "off" odour in the wine. These are the kinds of defects you are most likely to encounter:

- *Corked* is the most common flaw (the average occurrence is said to be about one in every 12 bottles). It's also the easiest to identify again when you've smelled it once. The wine gives off a musty, damp basement, or cardboard, smell.
  This is nearly always isolated to one bottle and not the whole shipment, but it can happen to any bottle that uses a cork. Don't drink corked wine; it's not harmful but it's not a pleasant experience.
- When wine is *oxidized*, it smells of dried-out fruit or sherry. The wine has been exposed to air, either because it wasn't stored properly or because the cork was defective. The problem could be isolated to one bottle, unless the whole case was stored improperly. If you taste the wine, it will seem flat or unusually weak. Don't drink it.
  If a wine becomes overly oxidized – very old or too much air was allowed in the barrel – the wine is said to be *madeirized*. The aromatics are reminiscent of madeira but with more cooked, dried-out molasses flavours. It's pretty hard to miss.
- When wine goes bad, it turns to *vinegar*. Because so many wines are treated with sulphur dioxide, it shouldn't happen but it does. And you'll know it. This is also probably isolated to one bottle. Don't drink it.
- A *sulphur* smell is a bacterial aroma often due to bad winemaking practices. You will recognize it as rotten eggs. It can affect a whole batch of bottles. Don't drink it even if you can get it past your nose.
- A common chemical aroma that can appear in wine is *acetone* (nail polish remover). Don't drink it.

Sulphur dioxide – the acrid smell of burnt matches – is less obnoxious than sulphur but isn't actually a fault. It's an antioxidant used by almost every winery to preserve the wine. It is more evident in younger wines. While it might be sharp enough to make you sneeze, it should dissipate after a few minutes.

There are many other odours that show up in wine but these are the more common ones and easiest to detect. They will also be the ones most familiar to people selling wine. This is important to know if you are returning the wine. Most wine stores will replace the defective wine no questions asked, assuming you have the sales receipt. Just make sure you return it close to full. Yes, they'll notice!

SAVING OPENED WINE

It isn't always possible to finish a whole bottle of wine at one sitting. Or maybe you have some left over from your dinner party. Instead of pouring it out, or sitting up all night drinking the dregs, here is what you can do to protect your opened wine:

- Use a hand-operated vacuum pump – Vacuvin is a common model – to remove the air. The pump comes with a rubber stopper with a one-way valve. You put the rubber stopper where the cork was, place the vacuum pump over it, and pump it a few times to create a vacuum. It helps delay oxidation and extends the life of your opened wine by a few days.
- A slightly more expensive option, but less labour intensive, is to use inert gas. Most wine shops sell this product in a canister – an extremely light canister that almost feels empty. You "spray" the odourless, tasteless gas, using a thin straw-like nozzle, into the top of the opened wine bottle. The gas displaces the oxygen, after which you push the cork back into the bottle. *Voilà* – the wine's life is extended by up to a week.
- The least expensive option is to transfer your partially full bottle into an empty, clean half bottle, then put the cork back in. Save a few half bottles when you come across them; they come in handy for this.
- Sparkling wines keep their fizz overnight in the fridge if you use a special wine stopper invented for this purpose, sold at most wine shops.

Whether you use the hand pump, inert gas, or the half bottle, put wine in the fridge to slow its decline even more. Eventually, though, the wine will lose its freshness and won't be as enjoyable as when you first opened it. Any wine opened for more than one week should be either used for cooking (but check first to make sure it hasn't gone bad) or thrown out.

WINE HAS STYLE

WHAT'S YOURS?

When we ask people what wines they like, they say things like, "A dry, light white wine with lots of flavour," or "Something rich and juicy . . . I love big red wines!" Body, sweetness, and flavour are all important ways to define your preference in wine – we call it the wine's style. Understanding what these terms mean will help you decide if you want something light enough to enjoy on a warm summer day or rich enough to stand up to your Mother's superb Sunday roast.

Now we're going to take everything you learned so far – grape variety, wine production, country of origin, and tasting – and pull it all together. That way you will be able to find the style you like, in a store, at a restaurant, or wherever you want to buy it.

WHAT'S IN STYLE?

Body, flavour, and sweetness are useful in defining a wine's style. These terms aren't unfamiliar – they are used in association with many other products – but how do they relate specifically to wine? And more importantly, how do they connect to the kind of wine you like?

Body

Body is about how a wine feels in your mouth. There are many ways to evaluate body but first, think about it in terms of *weight*. Alcohol, extracts (for example, sugars and tannins), and acidity are big contributors to the wine's body, and especially its weight:

- Lower-alcohol, dry white wines (e.g., Riesling) feel watery, or *light bodied*.
- Higher-alcohol, tannic red wines (e.g., Zinfandel) feel more *full bodied*.
- If the acidity is low, even lower-alcohol wines will feel *fuller*.

The difference in body isn't found only between white and red wines, however. For example, a German Riesling is much lighter bodied than a California Chardonnay. In this case it is because the Riesling is lower in alcohol than the Chardonnay. Beaujolais is lighter bodied than an Australian Shiraz. Here the difference is due to tannins (the Shiraz is more tannic), and perhaps alcohol content (the Shiraz being higher).

Another way to look at body is how the wine feels in your mouth in terms of *textures* (silky, velvety, or coarse) and *viscosity* (watery, thin, full, or thick). Think milk – skimmed milk, full fat milk, and cream – and you'll get the idea.

- Light-bodied wines (Pinot Noir) are silky.
- Medium-bodied wines (Merlot) coat your mouth more and are more velvety.
- Full-bodied wines (Shiraz) literally stick to your mouth and feel coarser, like wool.

What weight, textures, and viscosity appeal to you? Next time you drink a glass of your favourite wine, try to determine how you would classify it. Also think about the other foods and beverages you consume – are you consistent in your preferences?

Flavour

There are hundreds of different flavours in wine, but which ones appeal to you more? Knowing what you like in foods can help you determine your wine flavour profile. For example, do you like juicy, fruity foods? How about ripe or tart-tasting things? Do you prefer spicy, sweet, or savoury dishes? Do you prefer mild or intense flavours?

When deciding what flavours you prefer, it isn't important to be able to distinguish between a mandarin and a navel orange. All you need to know is that you prefer citrus fruits to tropical fruits, or that you prefer fruits in general over savoury things.

Perhaps when you drink a wine you don't want much flavour at all. That's okay; there are many neutral wines to choose from.

Dry to Sweet

Although you can't smell sweetness – sugar is not volatile – you can smell the aromas associated with sweet things. An off-dry Riesling, for example, gives off aromas of ripe peaches or apricots, while an unoaked Chardonnay (Chablis, for example) reminds us of lemons and wet stones. Peaches *smell* sweeter than citrus, and definitely sweeter than wet stones.

When you taste these wines, they will confirm what you thought when you took your first whiff. You will sense the sweetness in the off-dry Riesling, on the tip of your tongue, while the drier, almost tart Chablis will pucker your mouth.

Wines from warmer climates (Australia, for example) sometimes smell sweeter. If you like sweet things but prefer dry wines, then New World wines might be a good choice.

Alcohol also smells sweet, so more alcoholic wines, like Amarone, may suggest sweetness but in fact they are dry. And some high-alcohol wines, like Recioto, smell sweet because they are sweet. There's no hard and fast rule here, but there will be no doubt when you taste it.

FINDING YOUR STYLE

We all have our own threshold or preferences for body, sweetness, and flavour. What is light to one may be full bodied to someone else. People with a sweet tooth invariably find even off-dry wines too dry, and dry wines seem almost sour to them.

Price	Light-Bodied Wines	Medium-Bodied Wines	Full-Bodied Wines
Under £10	Chardonnay • Mâcon Blanc Sauvignon Blanc • Bordeaux Blanc • Chile Riesling • German Kabinett Muscadet Orvieto Soave Vinho Verde Verdicchio Vernaccia Pinot Grigio Liebfraumilch	Chardonnay • Mâcon-Villages • St-Véran • Montagny • Languedoc • Chile Sauvignon Blanc • Entre-Deux-Mers • California (Fumé Blanc) Pinot Blanc • Alsace Gewürztraminer • Chile • California	Viognier • California • Languedoc
£10 to £15	Riesling Sauvignon Blanc • Sancerre Chardonnay • Chablis • Petit Chablis • Mâcon-Villages Chenin Blanc Grüner Veltliner Orvieto Classico Muscat d'Alsace Torrontés	Sauvignon Blanc • Graves • Pouilly-Fumé • New Zealand Chardonnay • South Africa • California • Australia Riesling • Alsace • Australia Gewürztraminer Semillon • Australia Soave Classico Gavi Pinot Gris • Oregon • Alsace Verdelho	Chardonnay • Australia • California • Pouilly-Fuissé • Spain • Canada • Oregon • South Africa Viognier • Rhône
Over £15	Chardonnay • Chablis • Petit Chablis	Chardonnay • Chablis premier cru	Chardonnay • Chablis grand cru • Côte de Beaune • Burgundy premier and grand cru • California • Oregon • Washington • Australia Sauvignon Blanc • Pessac-Léognan • Marlborough (NZ)

Learn about the styles that appeal to you by trying wines in each category. We'll cover still wines first, followed by rosé, sparkling, fortified, and dessert wines. In the corresponding charts, the grape varieties that fit each body type are listed, along with some typical countries or regions that make "textbook" examples of these wines. Flavour profiles accompany each chart to help you determine what appeals to you.

Styles are matched to different price brackets. Expect finer textures from the more expensive wines – grand cru white Burgundy, for example, will feel more round and supple on the palate than a less expensive Chardonnay. Winemaking styles and grape ripeness can complicate this, though, so we are throwing it out only as a generalization.

Dry White Wines

There's a whole range of dry white wine styles to explore, from neutral to in-your-face attitude wines.

Fresh and crisp

When you need a wine to drink on its own or to build up an appetite for dinner, reach past the Chardonnay and grab a cool glass of tangy, fresh, crisp wine. Sounds like a commercial jingle for:

Entre-Deux-Mers	Riesling Kabinett	Verdicchio
Muscadet sur lie	Vinho Verde	Sancerre

Smooth and creamy

If tangy is just not right for you, perhaps you'd prefer something a little bit smoother. You'll likely pay a little bit more; these wines have probably seen the inside of an oak barrel at some time in their life. Look for:

Burgundy	Pessac-Léognan	Sémillon
Rioja	Pinot Blanc	Fumé Blanc

Would you like wood with that wine?

Some people prefer their white wine to be rich, ripe, and toasty. Watch for splinters:

Californian Chardonnay	Australian Chardonnay

Attitude whites

These aren't big, hit-you-over-the-head wines. Instead, they are distinctly aromatic. More often than not, they are actually light-bodied wines, but they pack some delightful fragrances. Check these out and you will see what we mean:

Gewürztraminer	Muscat d'Alsace	Viognier
Sauvignon Blanc	Torrontés	Verdelho

Neutral wines

Some people prefer white wines that don't smell of oak, tropical fruits, or "cat's pee." And there are occasions that simply call out for neutral wines. Think of a nice summer afternoon on a patio with a plate of oysters – organoleptic heaven! The Old World has cornered the market on this type of wine. Try these:

Verdicchio	Soave	Pinot Grigio
Orvieto	Muscadet	Vinho Verde

Dry Red Wines

For red wines you will find styles ranging from juicy to mellow to big and bold.

Fruity, mouth-watering reds

If you prefer your red wines packed with fruit and stuffed with mouth-watering acidity, and with very little tannins, there's a lot to choose from. Better still, you don't have to pay through the nose for them. Many of these red wines come from the Old World, the most famous being Beaujolais. Italy, however, really corners the market on juicy, mouth-watering reds. Here are a few other examples for you to try:

Barbera d'Asti	Dolcetto	Valpolicella
Bardolino	Chianti	Malbec (Argentina)

Smooth and silky

If you like your red wines to be more mellow and seductive, you may have to pay a little bit more, but we think you'll agree it is worth it. Give these wines a try:

Burgundy	Pinot Noir	Merlot
Chianti Classico	Rioja	Navarra

Attitude reds

For the extraverts in the group, how about some not-so-subtle wines – those hit-you-over-the-head, big, bold, and spicy wines? Although there are a few bargains out there, be prepared to pay a little more for these intense wines. Many of them will improve with age if you have the patience. If you keep them too long, though, they may mellow. In addition to Cabernet Sauvignon from Australia, California and, of course, Bordeaux, try these:

Australian Shiraz	Rhône Syrah	Zinfandel
Baco Noir	Barolo	Barbaresco

Price	Light-Bodied Wines	Medium-Bodied Wines	Full-Bodied Wines
Under £10	Merlot • Eastern Europe • Chile • Languedoc Cabernet Sauvignon • Bordeaux AC Pinot Noir • Bourgogne Rouge • Chile Gamay • Beaujolais Bourgogne Passetoutgrains Chianti Montepulciano D'Abruzzo Valpolicella Bardolino	Bordeaux supérieur Malbec Southern Italian reds Grenache • Australia • Côtes du Rhône • Italy • Spain Vin de Pays d'Oc	Bairrada Dão Pinotage Baco Noir
£10 to £15	Pinot Noir • Loire Cabernet Franc • Loire • Italy Côtes du Rhône Rioja Crianza Barbera d'Asti Dolcetto	Syrah/Shiraz • Crozes-Hermitage • Australia Pinot Noir • Burgundy Villages • Burgundy Côtes • Oregon Cabernet Sauvignon • Crus bourgeois • Haut-Medoc • Languedoc Cabernet/Shiraz Blends • Australia Merlot • Chile • California Gamay • Cru Beaujolais Zinfandel Rioja Reserva Rosso di Montalcino Barbera Valpolicella Classico Petite Sirah	Cabernet Sauvignon • Australia • South America Merlot • California Shiraz • Australia Zinfandel Vino Nobile de Montepulciano Barbaresco Châteauneuf-du-Pape
Over £15		Merlot • Saint Émilion • Pomerol Pinot Noir • Burgundy premiers cru • Burgundy grand cru • Oregon Rioja gran reserva Ribera del Duero Chianti Classico riserva Cabernet Franc • Saint Émilion	Cabernet Sauvignon • Bordeaux Châteaux • Napa, California • Washington State • South Australia Syrah/Shiraz • Hermitage • Côtes-Rôtie • Cornas Barolo Super-Tuscans Brunello di Montalcino Amarone Priorato Ribera del Duero

Rosé

Rosé has an image problem; it isn't considered to be a serious wine. People in the south of France, even the tourists, don't have this problem. Rosé wine is a way of life. There you will find a bottle on every table at lunch; it is more popular than white wine.

It might be White Zin – a sweetish blush wine from California – that turned many people off rosé. Good rosé should be light and dry, refreshing and low in alcohol – essentially the perfect wine for lunch.

The best grape for rosé is Grenache (Garnacha in Spain). It produces a wine with a slight mauve or pinkish orange hue in both a crisp and elegant style (Provence) or a slightly heavier, more alcoholic style (Navarra).

Here are some starting points for you if you want to give rosé a try:

Lighter Style	Heavier Style	Sweeter Style
Bandol	Tavel	White Zinfandel
Bordeaux	Spanish Rosado	Mateus Rosé
Cabernet d'Anjou	Clairet	Lambrusco

Sparkling Wine – It's Not Just for Breakfast Anymore

Most people don't think about what sparkling wine tastes like. They are too preoccupied with drinking it out of slippers or smashing it against the bows of ships. So why do we bother classifying sparkling wines? Why not just determine the price you are willing to pay?

There are different styles of sparkling wine, and as you drink more of them you will see that there is more to them than price and bubbles. The body of a sparkling wine is harder to determine than that of a still wine, as you have all those bubbles floating around to distract you. One of the easier ways is to look at the grape variety – as they do in Champagne (where they give body a lot of thought).

- Lighter-bodied sparkling wines (e.g., Blancs de Blancs Champagne) have more white grapes like Chardonnay in their blend
- Fuller-bodied sparkling wines (e.g., Blancs de Noir Champagne) have more black grapes like Pinot Noir in their blend.

Method of production (*méthode traditionelle* vs. tank), the length of time the wine rests on the lees, and the sweetness of the wine all have an effect on body. A secondary fermentation of over two years, as with vintage champagne, produces an elegant, rich wine that has millions of fine, and persistent, bubbles. When the fermentation of the wine is stopped before the sugars are converted to alcohol, and the secondary fermentation occurs quickly in a pressurized tank, the resulting sparkling wine is sweeter, with large, coarse bubbles that don't last very long in the glass.

Party Hint

If you are planning a stand-up reception with appetizers, choose a lighter-style sparkling wine. Fuller versions are better served at a meal where the wine may accompany a course or two.

In Champagne, each champagne house has its own *house style*, so you can pick the wines that match your style. And best of all, once you determine the style you like, there isn't much variation from year to year.

- Lighter-bodied house styles: Laurent-Perrier, Perrier-Jouët, Pol Roger, Pommery, Taittinger
- Full-bodied house styles: Bollinger, Heidseck, Krug, Veuve Clicquot

Other countries often use different base grapes in their blends and a variety of different production methods. Even those sparkling wines that use the same grape varieties as champagne, and the same methods, can't seem to get it exactly right. Nevertheless, there are still many excellent sparklers at all price ranges and preferences.

If you want bubbles but don't want to pay for them, try a sparkling wine from the "Cheap and Cheerful" list. If you want champagne but prefer not to pay the big money, try one or more of "The Pretenders." If you prefer your bubbles slightly sweeter, with dessert, we have included a category for these as well. Of course, we have also included the "Real Thing" – champagne – out of respect.

Cheap and Cheerful	The Pretenders	Sweeties	The Real Thing
Sekt (Germany)	Cava (Spain)	Asti (spumante)	Vintage champagne
Lambrusco (Italy)	Saumur brut (Loire)	Moscato d'Asti	Grand Marque NV
Prosecco (Italy)	Crémant (France)	Prosecco Dolce	champagne
	New World sparkling wine (California, New Zealand, Australia, and Canada)		NV champagne
	Franciacorta (Italy)		

Fortified

Fortified wines can be dry and tangy or sweet and warming. The first category are better served as an apéritif, or with soups or tapas, while the second are good to plonk down with in front of a roaring fire, or maybe with dessert.

Fortified wines don't have to be expensive. It is easy to find good wines for under £10. Better ports – the vintage ones – cost a lot more but they aren't for everyday drinking. Besides, since it's unlikely you will drink these wines at one sitting – remember, they are fortified – you'll get more mileage from one compared to a bottle of still wine. That's our rationalization, anyway, for drinking port and sherry as often as we can.

Dry and tangy
Sherry is the benchmark wine in this category. This surprises many people because they think sherry is a sweet wine – like Harvey's Bristol Cream or Cyprus sherry, which bears no resemblance whatsoever to the original from Spain.

Sherry is deliciously tangy and the best are made bone dry. Some versions come in small bottles, so you can experiment. Best of all, it's not expensive. Here's what to consider when buying sherry:

- *Fino* sherries are the palest, driest, and tangiest. Gonzalez Byass Tio Pepe is a fino sherry, but there are many other examples.
- *Manzanilla* is a type of fino sherry, but from a different area, and has a subtle, salty tang due to the coastal location of the solera.
- *Amontillado* is essentially an aged fino and has developed a darker colour and more toffee flavours.
- *Palo Cortado* is richer than an Amontillado but not as concentrated as an Oloroso.
- *Olorosos*, when well made, are fabulous. Dark and dry, they have lovely aromas of nuts, figs, and raisins. They are an excellent and unusual apéritif – surprise your friends but have lots on hand, as you'll probably be asked for seconds. There are sweet-style Olorosos but we prefer the drier versions.

Other dry and tangy fortified wines include Vin Jaune from the Jura region of France, two Madeiras called Sercial and Verdelho (which is off dry) from Portugal, and Sicily's Marsala Vergine – a dry version of this traditional sweetened wine. Montilla-Moriles, a neighbouring region to Jerez, produces wines similar in style to sherry but just not as popular.

Sweet and warming

Port from Portugal is the benchmark wine in this category. There are "ports" from Australia and South Africa, but they are much sweeter and more toffee-like than real port. Here's what to consider when buying port:

- *Ruby port* and *vintage character port* are the simplest and cheapest, so don't expect a lot from these wines. They are okay to have on hand, but drink them soon after purchase. They don't improve with age.
- *Tawny port* has more character than ruby port. Better still are the aged tawnies. Ten-year-old tawny is the most popular, and the extra price for 20 or 30-year-old tawnies doesn't make much sense. They are also meant to be consumed right away and have been filtered for you.
- *Colheita ports* are aged tawnies from a single vintage, and like tawnies they are not meant to age once they are bottled.
- *Late-Bottled Vintage port* (LBV) has some of the characteristics of *vintage port* but no sediment. These are good value, but they don't age. Drink up.
- *Vintage port* is the top rung. These are produced only in the best (declared) years and can be quite expensive. On top of that you may have to wait 20 or more years (after the vintage) before they're ready. Consult vintage charts to know when it's the best time to drink these wines. And don't forget to decant the bottle – these wines have a lot of sediment.

Other sweet and warming fortified wines include:

- *Bual* and *Malmsey* Madeira (Portugal). Bual is nutty and raisiny while

---

Attention Chocolate Lovers
Banyuls is probably the single best match for chocolate in the world. It might be hard to find, but worth searching for.

Malmsey – the sweetest of all Madeiras – is more toffee-like. Both have the characteristic Madiera tangy acidity that helps them keep a long time – sometimes decades.

- *Marsala* (Italy) comes in different styles and colours. Stick with Marsala *Superiore*, which has a richer honey, brown sugar sweetness.
- *Vins doux naturels* is what the French call fortified wines. The best of these is Banyuls made from Grenache in the Languedoc-Roussillon. Maury, Rivesaltes, and Rasteau are also Vins Doux Naturels.

There are numerous sweet sherries – the most famous is pale cream sherry – that fit better in this category than with their tangy cousins. Pedro Ximénez, the sweetest style of sherry, is so thick it is best saved as a topping for vanilla ice cream.

Màlaga, also from Spain, fits here as well as does Commanadaria from Cyprus. It's made sherry style from sun-dried grapes and offers up lovely sweet, honeyed, raisined flavours.

Wine as Dessert?

There was a time when sweet wines were more valued than dry wines. Now they are usually reserved only for special occasions. It's too bad because these rich and luscious dessert wines are a perfect way to end a meal, as a substitute for dessert or simply to savour around a fire on a cool autumn evening. Or if you are into foie gras, some sweet wines are a perfect accompaniment.

Compared to most still wines, sweet wines are not cheap; the top wines can easily cost hundreds of pounds. These wines improve and evolve in the bottle – some for decades, even centuries – if that is any consolation. And fortunately, since serving sizes are small – 1 or 2 oz (30–60 ml) – a bottle, even a half-bottle, goes a long way.

Dessert Wine Grapes
Riesling
Gewürztraminer
Vidal
Muscat
Chenin Blanc
Sémillon

The body and flavours of a sweet wine have as much to do with how the grapes were treated (left on the vine, air dried, botrytized, or left to freeze) as it does the grape type. Many of these wines are fuller bodied due to the higher alcohol levels and the extract (sugars). As a general rule, though, Riesling produces the lightest versions.

Don't be surprised by the high levels of acidity in dessert wines – that is why some of the best German sweet wines keep forever. Acidity is the perfect complement to the rich sweetness, and makes them less cloying.

An easy way to categorize dessert wines is by price. Less expensive wines tend to be lighter (in colour and body). More expensive wines, like icewine, tend to be fuller all around. Unfortunately, your biggest problem isn't choosing a dessert wine to try but rather finding them. Some shops carry only a few selections.

Starter sweeties

Late harvest (*Vendage Tardive* in French) are the key words to look for on the labels. Most of these cost under £15, will be fairly light bodied, and won't be too intense:

- Alsace Vendage Tardive.
- German Auslese Riesling.
- Muscat de Beaumes-de-Venise is probably the best starter dessert wine from the Old World and usually there is a fair bit of it around.
- Chile exports an interesting and inexpensive late harvest Sauvignon Blanc (Errázuriz) that is worth seeking out.
- For something different, Recioto della Valpolicella (Italy) is a red dessert wine.

Getting serious

As we move up in price the wines in this category may include some botrytized and icewine versions. What they all have in common is that they are rich and luscious.

In the £15 to £30 range, there's obviously more choice:

- California Orange Muscat
- Alsace Selection de Grains Nobles
- Australian Semillon or liqueur Muscats
- Canadian icewine
- German Beerenauslese Riesling
- Hungarian Tokaji Aszú
- Botrytized Sémillon/Sauvignon Blanc blends from Monbazillac, Loupiac, Ste-Croix-du-Mont, and Cadillac
- Vin Santo and Recioto di Soave DOCG from Italy

Serious sweeties

At over £30 – every drop unctuous nectar – some of these wines may be as difficult to find as they are to budget for. While the demand at this price point may be small, it is more of a supply issue – there's so little juice to work with there's simply very little made. If you can't justify the price for personal consumption, they do make excellent gifts. Here are a few examples:

- German Eiswein and Trockenbeerenauslese Riesling.
- Vouvray (Liquoreux), Quarts de Chaume, or Bonnezeaux from the Loire Valley in France.
- Sauternes and Barsac from Bordeaux, France.
- Tokaji Essencia, a rare wine from Hungary.

World's First Dessert Wine

The legendary Tokaji Essencia of Hungary is so rich in sugar that it can take decades just to ferment the must. The resulting wine is intensely aromatic (apricots, marzipan, orange peel, tea, spices . . .) with perfect acidity to balance its syrupy sweetness.

Tokaji was created over 400 years ago – centuries before the sweet wines of France and Germany were developed.

QUICK PICKS

Here are 20 wines to keep in the back of your mind. Consider them when you are in a rush to buy something on the way home from work.

These wines made our list because of their versatility – they go well with anything. They are all either light or medium bodied and have ample acidity. They will never overpower the food, and they still have enough fruit and flavour to stand on their own. Best of all, good examples of these wines can be found for under £10.

Twenty Wines under £10

Country	Sparkling Wines	White Wines	Red Wines
France		Entre-Deux-Mers Mâcon-Villages	Beaujolais-Villages Côtes du Rhône Chinon
Italy	Prosecco	Soave	Chianti Valpolicella Dolcetto
Germany		Riesling Kabinett	
United States		Sauvignon Blanc	Pinot Noir
Australia		Verdelho	Shiraz
New Zealand		Sauvignon Blanc	
Spain	Cava		
Chile		Sauvignon Blanc	Merlot

And for those of you with even more hectic lifestyles, here's only five things to remember:

- Riesling is versatile enough for even fusion foods.
- Sauvignon Blanc, with its good acidity and flavours, shows you are in the know.
- Pinot Noir is a great crossover wine – the wine to serve even if you are having fish, meat, *and* something vegetarian.
- Merlot is a crowd pleaser. Who doesn't like it?
- Italian wines in general. Chianti is another good crossover wine. It and Soave will be easy to find in most supermarkets.

A CASE OF WINE FOR A DESERT ISLAND

Often we sit around and think about what wines we hope we would have with us if we were marooned on a desert island. Or the case of wine we'd sneak onto *Survivor* if we had a chance – no beef jerky for us.

These are our personal favourites and shouldn't influence your own choices. And no money changed hands in compiling this list (though if any of the producers would like to send us a supply, that would be okay).

1. Sherry Dry Oloroso Don Nuño (Lustau)
2. 2000 Sancerre (Henri Bourgeois)
3. 1990 Riesling Haardter Herrenletten (Müller-Catoir)
4. 2001 Verdelho (Chestnut Grove)
5. 1996 Meursault Les Genevrières (P. Jobard)
6. 1996 Chambolle-Musigny (Ghislaine Barthod)
7. 1998 Pinot Noir Stripe Label (Blue Mountain)
8. 1997 Chianti Classico Riserva (Felsina)
9. 1990 Brunello di Montalcino (Castelgiocondo)
10. 1998 Cabernet Franc (Thirty Bench)
11. 1986 Bordeaux (Château Beychevelle)
12. 1995 Champagne Dom Perignon – for the rescue of course

CHILL OUT: TEMPERATURES FOR WINE

Regardless of the style of wine you prefer, it should be warm enough to bring out the flavours, yet cool enough to be refreshing but not chilling.

Temperature has a great effect on the aromas, body, and taste of wine and it's important to your overall enjoyment. Most people drink their white wines too cold and red wines too warm. When a white wine is served too cold, its true flavours are masked and the harsher elements – say, in an oaked Chardonnay – are emphasized. A red wine served too warm will taste unbalanced, as the alcohol and tannins will overpower the fruit flavours.

Sparkling wine, if not well chilled, will shoot out of the bottle like a geyser. So unless you just won a Formula One race, chill those sparklers. Dessert wines should also be slightly chilled.

Don't Bet the Spread

The temperature spread between red wines and white wines is actually much narrower than you may think. Light, fruity, low tannin red wines (e.g., Beaujolais) should be served at lower temperatures than full-bodied, complex white wines like grand cru white Burgundy. The list below is a guideline for ideal serving temperatures.

Medium to full-bodied reds	60–65°F (15–18°C)
Port or sweet sherries	55–60°F (13–15°C)
Full-bodied whites	55–60°F (13–15°C)
Light-bodied reds	50–55°F (10–13°C)
Rosé	50–55°F (10–13°C)
Light- to medium-bodied whites	50–55°F (10–13°C)
Dry sherries	45–50°F (8–10°C)
Sparkling wines	40–45°F (5–8°C)
Dessert wines	40–45°F (5–8°C)

White Wines – A Chilling Experience?

Refrigerators are simply too cold for white wines. In fact, you shouldn't let your wines near the fridge, except maybe to use the freezer as a quick chiller. A better method is to place the bottle in an ice and water mixture for a few minutes.

A temperature that's too low dulls the wine's aromas and neutralizes the taste. This may not be such a bad thing for simple wines, but it's your loss when you're about to open a good bottle you've been saving for a special occasion. If it is a sparkling wine, very low temperatures actually suppress the bubbles. (Fortunately, they come back as the wine warms up.)

In a restaurant, your white wine doesn't need to be kept in an ice bucket throughout the meal. That's as much for show as anything. If wine sits for only 20 minutes in an ice bucket, its temperature can drop about 20°F (10°C). Try drinking a glass of wine once it has reached 40°F (5°C) and it will freeze the enamel off your teeth.

If the restaurant is warm, you just need something to keep the wine's temperature constant. Some restaurants have clay or plastic bottle holders. Or drive your waiter crazy and simply keep moving the bottle between the table and the ice bucket.

Bad Fridge!

If left for a long time – weeks or even months – the low humidity in the fridge can dry out the cork. Your wines will either end up leaking in the fridge (and won't that be fun to clean up) or absorbing some interesting food odours. Imagine your nice bottle of Riesling coming out smelling like last night's leftover Chinese take-away!

Whose Room Temperature?

Red wines are supposed to be served at room temperature. Room temperature in a French Château (60°F/15°C), that is. If you have central heating, your room temperature (70°F/20°C) is too warm for red wines.

So if you have a cellar, leave the wine on the worktop for about 30 minutes before serving it. If you don't, take your room-temperature wine and chill it in the fridge for a few minutes before serving. Some lighter, juicy red wines like Beaujolais might benefit from an hour's time in the fridge.

Did You Know?

The average refrigerator temperature is 36–40°F (3–5°C).

Chilling a Sparkling Wine

Make sure your sparkling wines are well chilled before opening. When sparklers are properly chilled, the bottles are easier to open and the bubbles will last longer.

The one exception to this is vintage champagne, which needs to be treated more like a fine white wine and should not be served overly chilled. At the high end of the sparkling wine range, 45°F (8°C) is good.

Resist the temptation to cut corners. Don't chill the glasses to make up for a wine that's not chilled enough. The condensation on the glasses will dilute the wine and burst the delicate bubbles.

In a Hurry?

 Who isn't? Here are three ways to lower the temperature of a bottle of white wine from room temperature to serving temperature, and the amount of time it would take to do so:

- Ice and water – 20 minutes
- Freezer – 40 minutes (set a timer!)
- Refrigerator – three hours

If you have overchilled your wine, let the bottle stand on the worktop for a few minutes before opening. Wine will warm up about 2°F (1°C) every couple of minutes at room temperature, even faster if it is in a glass.

WOULD YOU LIKE WINE WITH THAT?

THE ART OF FOOD AND WINE MATCHING

"Red wine with red meat, white wine with fish." Most of us have heard this one. Follow the rule or risk some raised eyebrows from your waiter or even your table companions!

Contrast this school of thought with the approach, "Drink whatever wine you like with whatever you want to eat – there are no wrong combinations." Which approach is right?

Each one is, to a point. Rules provide guidelines to steer us toward more successful combinations. Spontaneity allows us to test the rules, maybe break them, and find some new ones that work. Here's one rule we hardly ever break, though: wine is meant to go with food.

Food and wine matches are all about finding a balance. Usually, you'll make your wine choices after you've decided on the menu. At other times, the wine will be the showcase of your meal.

Whatever your starting point, the following guidelines will give you options to explore. The old rules of wine and food matching were based on chemistry and logic, but above all, practice and experience. As you practice and gain experience with different wine and food combinations, your own palate will evolve.

As for the rules, you get to write the ones that work for you.

PRACTICAL PAIRING PRINCIPLES

Wine should make food taste better; food should make wine taste better. It's as simple as that. You don't need to be an expert to make great food and wine combinations. All you need to do is follow some basic guidelines:

- Match the weight of the wine to the weight of the food
- Adjust for the cooking method and for sauces
- Mirror ingredients but also look for contrasts
- Order makes a difference

Matching Weights

All foods have body and texture, a sense of how they feel in the mouth. Foods that are full of flavour, like a steak or Camembert cheese, almost coat your mouth when you eat them. Light-textured foods, like a green salad or poached fish, feel delicate and refreshing in the mouth.

The wines you choose to complement each dish must match the weight and texture of the food, neither overpowering the other. A steak wouldn't match a light-bodied wine, especially a light-bodied white wine. A full-bodied, full-flavoured bruiser wine like Shiraz would make a much more even match. However, the same Shiraz would just flatten poached fish. This dish needs a light-bodied white wine like Sancerre.

We have already classified wines into light, medium and full bodied. Here are some dishes that would go well with them:

Dry white wines

Light-Bodied Wines	Medium-Bodied Wines	Full-Bodied Wines
• Raw vegetables	• Prosciutto with melon	• Pâté
• Clear soups	• Vegetable soups	• Cream soups
• Green salad with a mild dressing	• Green salad with creamy dressing	• Warm mushroom salad
• Sushi	• Prawns or scallops	• Grilled salmon
• Poached fish	• Panfried fish	• Lobster
• Roast lemon chicken	• Chicken pie	• Roast turkey
• Steamed asparagus	• Stuffed peppers	• Grilled vegetables
• Pasta primavera	• Pasta with seafood	• Pasta in cream sauce
• Omelettes	• Quiche	• Eggs benedict
• Goat and other fresh cheeses	• Jarlsberg and other firm, mild cheeses	• Brie and other semi-soft cheeses

Dry red wines

Light-Bodied Wines	Medium-Bodied Wines	Full-Bodied Wines
• Pizza with seafood	• Grilled sausages	• Chicken and pork satays
• Lentil soup	• Winter vegetable soup	• French onion soup
• Grilled vegetable salad	• Warm chicken salad	• Grilled mushroom salad
• Deep-fried calamari	• Mixed grilled seafood	• Chicken cacciatore
• Fish with wine sauce	• Grilled tuna	• Barbequed chicken
• Grilled chicken	• Chicken stew	• Grilled lamb chops
• Hamburgers	• Grilled pork chops	• Steaks
• Pasta with pesto sauce	• Cheese or meat tortellini	• Beef stew
• Quiche	• Omelette with smoked salmon	• Vegetable lasagne
• Mild firm cheeses	• Parmigiano Reggiano	• Aged cheeses

Making Adjustments

The way food is prepared determines the intensity of its flavour. When it's steamed or poached, the flavour is very mild, even bland. Flavour picks up when the same food is fried or baked, and shifts up another notch when broiled, grilled, or slow cooked.

As cooking methods differ, the food's intensity changes, and so too does the need to match it with a bolder, fuller-bodied wine. The length of

Wine	Poaching or Steaming	Sautéing or Pan Frying	Deep Frying	Roasting	Grilling
Light-bodied whites	✓	✓	✓		
Medium-bodied whites		✓	✓	✓	
Off-dry whites		✓	✓	✓	
Full-bodied whites		✓	✓	✓	✓
Light-bodied reds		✓	✓		
Medium-bodied reds		✓	✓	✓	✓
Full-bodied reds				✓	✓

time something is cooked will also influence your choice of wine. Steak cooked rare goes best with a young tannic red wine; steak cooked well done, or even as a roast, is better suited to more mature, less tannic red wines. The tannins in the young wine bond with the proteins in the rare steak, making the wine taste much softer.

Here are some basic guidelines:

Thinking saucy

A change in sauces can re-balance the entire relationship between a food and a wine. Sometimes it's the sauce that dominates the dish. When we think of pasta, for example, we don't think of the shape – farfalle or bucatini – we think of the sauce: Alfredo, Primavera, Arrabiata, Marinara, and so on. Sauces can be light or rich, smooth or chunky, creamy or zippy.

Different wine styles complement different sauces. With a delicate sauce, choose a delicate wine. With a more robust sauce, pick a heartier wine.

Light-Bodied Wines	Medium-Bodied Wines	Full-Bodied Wines
• Pesto sauce	• Marinara	• Bolognese
• Lemon butter	• Velouté	• Béarnaise
• Chicken stir fry	• Chicken stew	• Barbequed chicken

Mirror, Mirror

Wines can also boost the flavour of a meal by mirroring its complexity: the simpler the meal, the simpler the wine.

Let's say you're planning to serve a simple grilled steak for dinner, with a fresh tomato salad and bread on the side. You need something equally simple to complement the meal, perhaps a light-bodied red wine like Chianti. Now, if this were a pepper steak, served with red pepper and ginger marmalade, the slightly sweet and spicy accompaniment and the peppery coating on the steak now dominate the dish and would overpower the Chianti. You would need something with a flavour profile that would work with the sauce. Full-bodied wines with peppery undertones like Syrah (Shiraz) or a Zinfandel would work well. Fruitier accompaniments, like a papaya salsa, would be better suited to a wine with more tropical aromas, like New Zealand Sauvignon Blanc.

Wine	Has Undertones Of	Suits
Old World Sauvignon Blanc	Herbs	Herb vinaigrette
Oaked Chardonnay	Creamy	Garlic mayonnaise
Red Burgundy	Earthy	Mushroom sauces
Riesling	Fruit	Chutney
Rosé	Fruit	Cranberry
New World Sauvignon Blanc	Tropical fruits	Salsa (e.g., papaya)
Syrah/Shiraz	Spices	BBQ, pepper sauces
Cabernet Sauvignon	Mint	Mint sauce
Muscat	Orange	Fruit sauce

The aroma and flavour profiles of the wines we covered earlier will help you identify other wine matches for different styles of sauces. Here are a few examples:

Opposites attract
Sometimes wine works best when it provides a contrast to the food, rather than a complement. Tannins and acidity in a wine can offset fat, its fruit flavour can moderate spiciness, and its sweetness can balance saltiness.

In food terms, think of fish and chips. Some people like to intensify the richness of the chips by dipping them in mayonnaise. Others like the contrast of vinegar on the fried food, cutting through its greasy goodness. Still others slather the whole meal in ketchup, enjoying the contrast between salt and sweet.

Contrasting food and wine works much the same way.

- Creamy-textured, rich, or fatty foods cut the tannins in wine (for example, a young Chilean Cabernet Sauvignon), allowing the fruit flavours in the wine to show through.
- Acidity, in a German Riesling, for example, cuts the fattiness in fried foods – filo pastry appetizers, pork chop, deep-fried anything – just like a squeeze of lemon would.
- The sweetness in a wine counters the saltiness of food. Likewise, the saltiness of food makes the wine's flavours stand out even more. Sweetness in wine also cools the heat of spicy foods. An off-dry Gewürztraminer is a great match for Thai or Indian curries.

Hooked on classics
Most of the tried and true food and wine combinations originate from Old World countries like France, Italy, and Spain. There, they've had centuries to develop and perfect their regional cuisines and wines to bring out the best in each other.

Here are some of those classic combinations:

- **Champagne and caviar** – The cooling, refreshing acidity and bubbles of the wine contrast with the salty richness of the fish eggs.
- **Dry Oloroso sherry and consommé** – The rich nutty aromas of the wine complement the intense earthy aromas of the soup.

- **Sancerre and chèvre** – The acidity of the wine complements the tangy acidity in the goat cheese. Matched together, the acidity of each is actually toned down.
- **Barolo and braised beef (osso buco)** – The exotic aromas of the wine complement the flavours in long-roasted meat.
- **Cabernet Sauvignon and grilled steak** – Okay, maybe this is more of a New World classic. The heavyweight wine complements the big, smoky meat.
- **Sauternes and foie gras** – The rich, syrupy texture of the wine complements the rich, silken fattiness of the liver; the sweetness of the wine contrasts with the liver's savoury flavour.
- **Port and Stilton** – The fullness of the wine complements the fullness of the cheese; the sweetness of the wine contrasts with the saltiness of the cheese; and the bitter tannins in the wine counteract the bitterness in the blue veins.

And now for something new

The old rules of food and wine matching still make sense. But they were established in the days of regional cuisines, when French foods could be matched only with French wines, Italian foods with Italian wines, and so on.

New rules are being created all the time. Pinot Noir, a red wine, is now accepted as a perfect match for salmon. The acidity in the wine cuts through the fattiness in the fish; the weight of the wine and the food complement each other. A big, fully oaked Chardonnay with a well-done steak? Why not? For many cuisines – Thai, Japanese, or Indian, for example – wine is not part of the mealtime ritual, and there are no time-tested food and wine combinations. So we are free to experiment. How about Australian Verdelho with spring rolls, sparkling wine with sushi, or Beaujolais with curry?

Now that we also have access to quality wines from all points of the globe, we also have the freedom to adapt the classic food and wine combinations. If Sancerre and chèvre work well together, shouldn't New Zealand Sauvignon Blanc work just as well with goat's cheese? Why not substitute a dessert wine like icewine for the classic port and blue cheese combination?

Here are some new combinations to try:

Food Style	Wines
Brunch – egg dishes	Sparkling wines
Chinese	Dry Riesling, Gewürztraminer (off dry if Szechuan-style)
Indian	Rosé, Beaujolais
Japanese	Off-dry Riesling, Gewürztraminer, sparkling wines
Mexican	Sauvignon Blanc, Malbec
Fusion	Unoaked Chardonnay, Pinot Noir
BBQ	Riesling, Zinfandel, Shiraz
Thai	Riesling, Sauvignon Blanc, Verdelho
Death by chocolate dessert	Orange Muscat

Order Makes a Difference

There are a few basic principles for serving wine with a meal:

- **Dry before sweet** – Dry wines, especially ones with some acidity, prepare your palate for food. They stimulate the appetite, as do sparkling wines, and enhance the kinds of foods served early in a meal. Sweetness lingers on the palate and makes it difficult to appreciate a dry wine following it. Sweet wines close the palate and end the meal.
- **Light before full** – Think of all of the components that make a wine taste full bodied: alcohol, sugar, tannins, glycerin. If you serve a light-bodied wine after a full-bodied one, it will taste weak and watery by contrast.
- **Young before old** – Young, simple wines are the warm-up act for older, more complex wines. Usually when more than one wine is served over the course of a meal, the oldest (and presumably best) one is reserved for the main course.

The "white wine before red wine" debate is more about the colour of wines and doesn't take into account body, sweetness, flavour, or even age. For example, we would serve Beaujolais before a full-bodied Chardonnay. It's one rule that makes sense to break.

Pudding wines

 A number of wines can be used to end a meal, either with a cheese course or to accompany dessert. We have touched on some of them already. Here are a few more:

- **Cheese** – Dry red wines work well with hard cheeses. Sweet wines and fortified wines, like port, work best with aged blue cheeses. Here are some classic matches: Brie and Beaujolais, blue and port, cheddar and Syrah, chèvre and Sancerre, and Parmigiano Reggiano and Valpolicella.
- **Apple pie** – Off-dry white wines, like Riesling Auslese or Vouvray, will go well.
- **Cakes** – Moscato d'Asti, Madeira, Orange Muscat, or tawny port.
- **Cheesecake** – Off-dry Gewürztraminer or any medium-bodied white wine, preferably with a touch of sweetness.
- **Dark chocolate mousse** – Port or vins doux naturel.
- **Fruit tarts or fresh fruit** – Demi-sec sparkling wine or icewine.

Knowing the Limits

Not everything works with wine. No matter how hard you try, some wines and foods are on a collision course:

- **Salty foods** – Highly salted foods clash with the tannins in wine and make the wine taste bitter, astringent, and sometimes even metallic. Salt also emphasizes the taste of the alcohol in wines. Try lower-alcohol, fruity white wines with a touch of residual sugar instead.

> *A Pinch Is Okay*
> A little bit of salt on your meal will soften the astringency in a tannic red wine.

- **Spicy foods** – Hot and spicy foods accentuate the alcohol in most wines, sort of like throwing petrol on a fire. Try low-alcohol, fruity white wines – Moscato d'Asti or German Riesling – or a low-tannin fruity red wine like Beaujolais. Serve slightly chilled. If all else fails, there's always cold beer.
- **Acidic and pickled foods** – Extremely acidic foods can make wine taste flat and sweet, even unpleasantly sweet. Artichokes, for example, are so acidic they even make water taste sweet. But when acid in food – even vinegar-based salad dressings – is matched with acidity in wine (for example, Sauvignon Blanc), the overall perception of acidity is lowered and the other flavours in the food and wine show through.
- **Unfermented dairy products** – Medium- to high-acid wines are not recommended for butter or cream-based sauces as they will make the food taste rancid.
- **Fish and red wine** – Some red wines work with seafood, but many don't, hence that old rule. The tannins in red wine clash with the iodine and other components in seafood, and the result is a nasty metallic taste. With salmon or other fatty fish, lower-tannin, low-alcohol red wines such as Pinot Noir, Barbera, and Beaujolais work well. Grill, or blacken the fish to bring out a "meatier" taste and texture. Acidity (like a squeeze of lemon) is a good counter to the fishiness of oysters, sushi, or other shellfish. Stick to unoaked, crisp, light-bodied, white wines like Chablis, Muscadet, and even sparkling wine.

  > *Wine's Worst Enemies*
  > Artichokes
  > Asparagus
  > Spinach
  > Vinegar
  > Eggs

- **Meat and white wine** – If we're talking about a big, juicy steak, grilled to perfection, then most white wines, or even a light-bodied red wine, will taste like little more than lemon juice and water next to it. If you prefer white wine to red, poultry, veal, and pork (especially when accompanied by sweet or spicy sauces) are better matches. With a big rare steak, stick to red wine. If the steak is well done then it's okay to try an oaky Chardonnay – think Californian.
- **Eggs** – Wine may not be the first thing that comes to mind when you think of breakfast. But what about brunch or egg dishes like omelettes? Eggs are delicate but with sufficient fat content – in the yolks or the sauces – to create a problem. Stick with light-bodied, low-acid, neutral white wines, sparkling wines, or very light-bodied red wines. Beaujolais goes well with omelettes and Alsace Riesling or Sylvaner is a classic match for quiche.
- **Sweet desserts** – If you're ending the meal with a sweet dessert, always make sure the wine you choose is sweeter. Ice cream and tropical fruits can't be out-sweetened by wines, so avoid matching them up.
- **Chocolate** is a special problem. Its sweet intensity and body make it a tough match – but not impossible. Sweet Muscats, Banyuls, and ruby or tawny port are worth a try. Cabernet Sauvignon is a good match with dark chocolate. You could also try icewine, but it's really a dessert unto itself.

NEVER COOK WITH WINE YOU WOULDN'T DRINK

If a wine doesn't taste good in the glass, don't cook with it. All flavours in a wine, good or bad, are intensified once the wine is heated. Here are some general guidelines for cooking with wine:

- **Use blends** – Fruity, medium-bodied wines that are made from a blend of grapes (Côtes du Rhône, for example) contribute more complex, well-rounded flavours than single-varietal wines.
- **Avoid oak** – Sauces made with heavily oaked wines (e.g., Cabernet Sauvignon) may develop astringent, bitter, and sometimes harsh tastes.
- **Use wine as a bridge** – The wine you cook with should be of the same style or grape variety as what you are drinking. This forms a bridge between the wine in the glass and the wine in the sauce.
- **Use wine to flavour the food** – Use wine as you would herbs and spices, to bring out other flavour dimensions in the meal. You can also use wine to tenderize, colour, baste, and as a base for sauces.
- **Cook off the alcohol** – When cooking with wine, use low, slow heat to evaporate the alcohol, leaving only the flavour of the wine behind. Rapid heating of a wine will result in a sauce that is tart and murky. "Raw" wine is rarely used in a dish.

WINE FOR ALL SEASONS

Like foods, wines have a "season." That light-bodied Riesling you happily enjoyed on the patio last summer may not be as comforting as a glass of Amarone or port in front of the fireplace in the wintertime. Just as salads and sandwiches keep us cool when the weather is hot, and soups and stews warm us up on winter days, your choice of wines will vary over the course of the year.

Here are suggested menus and wine matches geared to the seasons:

Spring

Menu Items	Wine Suggestions
Lamb cutlets Scalloped potatoes Courgette and red pepper compote Raw fennel and apple salad Pineapple upside-down cake	• If you were going to go with one wine, try a Riesling or a rosé with a hint of residual sugar. • For reds, try a lightly chilled Beaujolais, Barbera, or Dolcetto. • Sauvignon Blanc would complement the courgette and fennel. • Maybe a Moscato d'Asti with dessert.

Summer

Menu Items	Wine Suggestions
Raw crudites with white bean basil dip Grilled herbed chicken with aioli Hamburgers Potato salad Watermelon or chocolate ice cream	• For a single crossover wine, a lightly chilled Dolcetto, Cabernet Franc (Loire), or rosé would go well. • Sauvignon Blanc or Pinot Blanc would work with the crudites and chicken dishes. • Tawny port or Oloroso sherry with the chocoloate ice cream, but not the watermelon.

Autumn

Menu Items	Wine Suggestions
Turkey with all the trimmings Mashed potatoes Roasted root vegetables Steamed broccoli and cauliflower Apple pie	• There's an undercurrent of sweetness in this traditional meal. • Off-dry Gewürztraminer or Riesling would work well. Even a full-bodied rosé would be okay. • Zinfandel is a good choice for a red wine. • Late harvest Riesling or Gewürztraminer with the pie.

Winter

Menu Items	Wine Suggestions
Beef stew Roasted root vegetables Chocolate mousse	• For a red wine, try Rioja, something from the Côtes du Rhône, or a Syrah/Shiraz to match this hearty meal. • Most white wines (except maybe Alsace Pinot Gris) will be too light bodied for this menu. • Maybe a glass of port or Banyuls with dessert.

BUYING WINE IN A RESTAURANT

Restaurant wine lists, on the whole, are not exactly user friendly. Although this is changing, more often than not they are grouped by type of wine: sparkling, white, red, and dessert wines, but after that, all bets are off.

Most lists are organized by country, while others group wines by grape variety – Chardonnay, Sauvignon Blanc, Cabernet Sauvignon, and so on. The restaurants that use these formats expect that you know what these wines are, where they are from, and if the vintage is good, in order to select them.

Some wine lists include a section for special and expensive wines, called the "reserve list." This is always fun to look at, like window shopping at a Porsche dealership.

Carved in Stone
If the wine list is laminated and you don't see any vintages listed, don't expect any great finds.

Kudos to those restaurants that organize their lists by style, from light and crisp white wines to robust, full-bodied red wines. It makes it so much easier to select a wine that you aren't familiar with or to try something unique. The restaurant might even suggest certain food–wine matches, which is great since they should know their own food the best.

A wine list organized by price, preferably in ascending order, makes it easier to find a wine that matches what you are planning to spend. We've even seen wine lists that are organized by price point: under £10, £15-30, and so on. These are great if you want to compare different wine styles within a specific range.

Finally, restaurants that want your business indicate vintages and actually have the wines available that are on the list. There is nothing more frustrating than picking a wine to match your meal only to find, "We don't carry that wine any more, sir." A restaurant can redeem itself, however, by offering a suitable alternative at the same price.

Ordering Wine with Confidence

Here's a quick five-step process for ordering wine in a restaurant with confidence:

Step 1
Look at the food menu and discuss what you and your fellow diners want to eat. See if there are any strong preferences for certain wines. If more than one of you wants to help choose the wine, ask for another copy of the list.

The Dilemma

In The Opening we described a scenario to you: what wine to pick with salmon, a vegetarian dish, and pork? What would you recommend?

We'd go with a crossover wine like Pinot Noir or Chianti. Both have sufficient body, flavour, and acidity to make a great match. You should find one for under £20 on most restaurant wine lists.

Step 2

Agree on what you want to spend. If you are having more than one bottle, keep that in mind, too. A regular 750 ml bottle of wine gives you about five glasses of wine. Scan the wine list to see what's available in your budget range. Look at the kinds of wines you like, what matches the food you want to eat, and the prices. Don't be rushed, take as much time as you need to choose the wine.

Step 3

Don't worry about remembering vintage years because most restaurants sell the current vintage available. You probably won't have much of a choice. If you want to order a more expensive bottle you might want to ask for some advice about the vintage. If you have a vintage card in your wallet, it never hurts to sneak a peek, just to make sure the sommelier's recommendation matches what others have said about the year.

Step 4

Stick with the wines that match the restaurant's food theme. You might love Australian Shiraz, but at Tony's Pasta Express it's a good bet the Chiantis are *bellissimo*!

Step 5

If the restaurant has a sommelier (the name will probably be written at the bottom of the wine list), ask him or her to recommend a few options. But first point out what you were considering as a choice, so he or she will have an idea of your budget. Also have an idea of what you and your guests are planning to eat, as the sommelier will likely ask.

Wine Picks by Restaurant Type

In Step 4 we recommended sticking with wines that match the restaurant's food theme. Here's a quick reference on what to order in different types of restaurants. It's likely you will find at least one of these suggestions on the wine list. If not, refer back to the guidelines on food and wine matching from the last section.

When in doubt, think, "When in Rome, do as the Romans do." You're always wise to stick with the local wines, especially when you're in a restaurant from a country with a strong wine and food culture. Of course, when you are travelling, you may not have any option but to follow this rule – don't expect to see your favourite Californian Cab in a Marbella tapas bar.

In This Type of Restaurant	Go for These Kinds of Wine
Italian	Simple Chianti or Valpolicella for pizza and pasta. Splurge on Brunello di Montalcino or an Amarone if it's a special occasion.
French	Match regional dishes with regional wines – for example, Muscadet with moules frites or Sancerre with fish; red Burgundy with casseroles; aged Bordeaux with simple grilled meats; Provençal wines with Mediterranean-style dishes; and champagne with everything.
Bistro	Look for village wines from the southern Rhône, Provence, or Languedoc-Roussillon. These wines can be a steal.
Sushi	Try the traditional – sake, which is actually closer to beer than wine. Otherwise, try Riesling or an unoaked Chardonnay like Chablis. Champagne is perfect if you're splurging.
Indian	The spice in Gewürztraminer complements exotic spices; low-alcohol, off-dry Riesling tempers spicy hot foods.
Steakhouse	Any warm climate Cabernet Sauvignon on the list – Californian or Australian, the bigger the better. Northern Rhône Syrahs or Australian Shiraz are better for pepper steaks.
Chinese	Not known for the wine selection. Stick with whites, preferably Riesling or Gewürztraminer. You might even see Blue Nun!
Thai	Sauvignon Blanc to enhance the lemongrass and herbal flavours; aromatic Rieslings from Australia; soft, fruity Pinot Blanc from Alsace.
Tapas	Dry sherries like fino or Oloroso sherry; rosé wines from Navarra; Rioja with anything grilled.
Seafood	Muscadet or Chablis with mussels or oysters; Sauvignon Blanc for light fish dishes; oaked Californian Chardonnay with lobster or salmon.
Fusion	Crossover cuisine calls for crossover wines. Try unoaked Chardonnays, Sauvignon Blancs, New World Pinot Noirs, Chianti, Dolcetto, or Beaujolais.

Am I Paying Too Much?

When you buy a bottle of wine at a restaurant, what you're really paying for is careful cellaring (you hope), clean, well-sized glasses (or at least bigger than the water glass), and the overall experience of being served. How much is that worth? That's up to you to decide. Some restaurants charge a small markup and others charge two to three times what the wine costs retail.

If you want to be pampered, you will have to pay for it. If you are on a budget, look for restaurants that charge a small markup or offer alternatives.

Alternatives
If you want to have wine with your meal, and the wine list is above your budget or you are eating alone, there are a number of other options available to you:

- **House wines** – We'd like to think that most restaurants carefully chose their house wine to reflect their menu. The reality is that many are chosen for their price point, their availability, and being least likely to offend anyone (which isn't always the case). If the restaurant cares about their wine list then they should also care about their choice of house wine.

  Most restaurants have at least two house wines: one white and one red wine. They may have a couple of choices for each, so ask what they are. A glass of house wine is usually a 6 oz (180 ml) serving, and a half-litre is about three glasses worth and should cost a little more than half the price of a full bottle. Ask to try a sample of the house wine, and if you like it, order it.

- **Wines by the glass** – Not all restaurants offer this option – we wish more would – and again we find that the better the wine list, the better the wine by the glass. You can order something specially selected by the restaurant, and some restaurants have been known to even open a bottle from the regular wine list to give you a glass. Ordering wines by the glass gives you the flexibility to match different wines to each course or the different wine preferences of your guests.

  Ask if the restaurant has a wine preservation system. If they don't, the bottle may have sat open for a few days, especially in a slow week. Don't accept wine if it hasn't been stored properly – ask for a sample to see if the wine is in good condition. As with a full bottle, it's your right to be served a perfect glass of wine.

  If a few of you are ordering the same wine by the glass, you may be better off splitting a full bottle. An added bonus with ordering a bottle is that you know the wine will be fresh.

- **Half bottles** – This is the sign of a restaurant that caters to its customers (especially those who dine alone.) Half bottles are cheaper than full bottles and reduce the tendency to overindulge. Half bottles are great even if there are two of you and you want to try one wine with your appetizer and another with your main course. Dessert wines often come in half bottles.

  As a rule, half bottles age much faster than large bottles, so try to buy more recent vintages.

- **Odds and ends** – Ask if they have other wines that are not on the list – not the expensive "reserve list," though! They may have changed the wine list recently and have a few odds and ends to clear out. If you are interested in any of the wines, ask for prices and make an offer. If you are a regular customer, they may bring in special wines for you at good price points.

- **BYO** – If you are lucky enough to live in an area where BYO (Bring Your Own) is allowed, you've got the best of all worlds. BYO allows you to bring in a bottle of your own wine and be charged only a "corkage" fee for having someone else serve it.

Getting the Right Service

Most waiters are trained to open and serve wine ordered by customers. But they don't always have the training, or the experience, to help you *choose* a wine.

Sommeliers go a step beyond. They are wine professionals, there to enhance your dining experience. They help you make a wine selection that will bring out the best in the food and the wine combined.

They can also be very intimidating, although most of the ones we know aren't. Remember, their job at the restaurant is to enhance your dining experience, not ruin it. The more you know about wine, even when you know just a little more, the less intimidating the relationship will be. Sit back and let the sommelier guide you through the meal.

You may be concerned about being pressured into buying something outside your price range. Don't be. Just ask for advice, and be clear about the style and price range. Give examples of the kinds of wine you most enjoy (brand names or styles). If you're with guests and don't want to talk prices, just use the list and point to some wines you were "thinking about" when asking for assistance.

Some restaurants have larger-sized, crystal glasses that they would be happy to provide if you request them. Whenever we've asked, the server has always been able to find something bigger and better than the ones that were on the table when we arrived. Don't forget to show your appreciation for the extra attention.

Even if you don't want – or need – the sommelier to be part of your wine decision, you still benefit from his or her expertise. The sommelier is the one who selects the wines for the restaurant, organizes and designs the wine list, and helps to train the other waiters. The best sommeliers are entertainers, diplomats, and, of course, a tremendous wealth of knowledge. Tap into it.

Check the label

Once you've got over the hurdle of ordering, it's wine time. As if ordering the wine isn't bad enough, this is when the pressure really builds for many people.

Before the cork is even pulled, the sommelier or waiter should present the wine to you, if you're the host. This is to make sure the wine is the one you ordered, and the vintage you expected. Don't simply glance at the bottle – it's hard to explain after you receive the bill that you weren't pointing to the '61 Lafite Rothschild on the wine list.

Then comes the grand opening. As intimidating as this whole process can be for you, for many waiters it can also be nerve-wracking. Imagine what you would feel like if you had to open a bottle of wine in front of a table full of staring people.

In many European restaurants they will not present the cork to you. The waiter inspects it, then discreetly tucks it away into a pocket – frustrating if you like to keep corks as a memento.

If you get the chance to check the cork, there are some clues you can discover from the condition of the cork that will alert you to the condition of the wine:

Cork Condition	Why	Remedy
Completely dry	Wine not stored on its side	• Probably okay if wine is young and simple • One sniff of the wine will confirm if it's oxidized
Soaked through	Wine stored on its side a long time	• Probably okay if an old wine • One sniff of the wine will confirm if it's oxidized or "over the hill."
Broken	Poor corkscrew technique or tightly fitted cork	• The wine will be okay, but you'll probably need a new bottle. A skilled sommelier will handle the problem without your having to ask.

Just glance at the cork to pick up these clues. You don't need to touch or sniff it. The cork is only an indicator; the real proof will come in the tasting.

If the wine needs to be decanted for sediment, the server will do so at this stage, before the tasting ritual.

To taste or not to taste?
Once the cork has been pulled, or the wine has been decanted, the waiter should pour a small sample of wine for the person who ordered the wine to taste. An interesting ritual and one that sends shivers up the spines of most novice wine drinkers. What to do?

In some restaurants, they do take the pressure off you. The sommelier pours a splash of wine in a glass and smells it to make sure it is of good quality before serving it to you. They have the training to do this and you should trust their judgement.

At many restaurants, however, waiters aren't really wine savvy. Your wine knowledge, as limited as it may feel to you, may far exceed that of the person serving you. Besides, you're the one paying for the wine.

So what *do* you do? Remember the Four S's? First, look at the wine and make sure it's clean and doesn't have anything weird floating in it. Next, sniff – this should tell you enough about its condition to make a decision. The tasting step confirms it all, but you don't have to taste a wine that you think is off. If you do taste the wine, we never recommend spitting in restaurants; it's better to swallow.

If you think there's a problem with the wine, indicate what you think it is. Ask one of your tablemates to join in to give you moral support. Defective wines are rare but when you come across one that is musty (corked), flat and flavourless (oxidized), or smells of sulphur, acetone, or vinegar, you don't have to accept it. Send it back. The restaurant should willingly replace the defective bottle with an alternative one without question.

Of course, don't expect to return a good wine that you just don't like. How this is handled is up to the discretion of the restaurant. We know a number of restaurants that have the policy, "If you don't like the wine, we'll replace it." This practice should be praised and supported but never abused.

When the wine is poured
If you think the wine is in good condition, ask the waiter to pour for the rest of the guests. If it's a white wine, check the temperature and ask for an ice bucket if it isn't chilled properly – don't let the waiter pour it right away.

The waiter should apportion the wine so that everyone who wants wine gets some, plus there should be some left in the bottle. The waiter should not fill the glasses more than half full.

Now, if you do decide to order another bottle of the same wine, you won't need new glasses for everyone. But you will need to make sure the second bottle is as good as the first. Don't let the waiter simply top up glasses of good wine with one that could be bad. The waiter should bring a clean glass so someone can taste the wine from the new bottle. We've forgotten this before, and it's an easy step to miss when you are engrossed in table conversation.

That's all you really need to know. Sit back, relax, and enjoy your meal.

BUY, BUY WINE

HELLO EMPTIES

The day has finally come to buy wine. But where to start? How much to spend? Where can you find what you want? And who do you ask if you can't find the wine you want?

WHERE CAN I BUY WINE?

Some of you are luckier than others with respect to what you can buy and where, how, and when you can buy it. Every country has different laws governing the sales of wine and spirits. Since we don't know where you live, we'll leave these details up to you, but here are a few of the options:

- **Retail** – This can include wine shops, supermarkets, and discount warehouses.
- **Wineries** – Although there are local laws governing this, you may be able to ship directly from a winery. Some wineries have mailing lists, or allocation lists, where they sell their more limited wines.
- **Online** – This is an increasingly popular option (if the online retailers can stay in business), but may also be controlled by local shipping laws. Buying online can be exciting but you may not want to risk shipping your wine across the country in July.
- **Auctions** – The best option for finding older wines.
- **Wine clubs** – An option for hard-to-get wines. Wine clubs, especially those that offer mail order, are perfect for people who live in remote rural locations and don't have the selection available in larger cities.

HOW MUCH TO SPEND?

A single bottle of wine can sell for £5 or for £500. Both are packaged in similar 750 ml bottles, both have a paper label, and both, of course, contain wine. We know the £500 version will taste better, but will it taste 100 times better?

Since not many people regularly buy £500 bottles of wine, the question is perhaps moot. But what about the difference between a £3 bottle and a £10 bottle? That's where it gets tricky. Decide how much money you want to spend, then get the *best* bottle of wine you can for that amount.

Value versus Quality

What can you expect to pay for a decent bottle of wine in a store?

- **Under £10** – The wine should show something of the character of the grape – a Merlot that tastes like Merlot, for example. Once in a while you will come across a Petite Sirah from Mexico or a Bulgarian Cabernet Sauvignon in the under-£5 range. If it's a grape type you already like, go ahead and try it. There are New World wines in this bracket as well as Old World wines. Old World wines will be mainly from the regional and table wine categories, and Vin de Pays d'Oc wines are particularly good bets.

  Wines in this price range are not always well made, however, so it's important to get a personal recommendation – ideally from a trusted source.
- **£10–£20** – As you climb up the price scale, the wine should be even more true to its variety and type. These wines are more concentrated, and they linger longer on your palate after you've swallowed them. They are polished, complex, and have a nice textured finish. A good, long finish is one of the extra benefits you get with a more expensive wine.

  There is a lot available in this range from both the New World and the Old World. You can expect to find Old World wines in the Quality category but not necessarily at the very top. Don't expect too many reserve or single-vineyard wines at this price.
- **Above £20** – Now you are either paying for a wine that's in limited supply, made with no expense spared, or from a good vintage. Or you're paying for the name of the winery or winemaker. Sometimes you pay for all four – these wines will have been lovingly cared for from the vine to the finished wine. Some wineries produce only one barrel's worth of a particular wine. That's only 300 bottles, or 25 cases!

  There is little dispute that these are high-quality wines, especially those that are made by a well-respected producer in a very good vintage. Almost every major winemaking region in the world makes wines in this price range. Bordeaux classed growths or California "cult" wines start around £100 when released and can cost thousands later through auction.

When you decide to pay top price for a wine, you want to know if it will be worth it. Here are some clues to look for:

- **Location, location, location** – Better wines tend to have the region or the vineyard identified on the label (e.g., Le Montrachet). The more specific the location – a vineyard is better than a region – the better the wine. Words like cru and clos (French), vigna and sori (Italian), and Grosslage and Einzellage (German) indicate the wine is from a specified vineyard.
- **Winemaker** – The best winemakers take what nature gives them in the grapes and express it through their particular style. They make good wines in even difficult vintages. Ask your wine shop for some names of reputable winemakers or read wine magazines.
- **Reserve** – This can be a sign of excellent quality or just a marketing term. These wines – the word "reserve" will appear somewhere on the label – should be made from grapes grown in the winery's best

---

Flying Winemakers
Some winemakers travel around the world consulting to different wineries in different countries. This was a name originally given to the Australian winemakers who came to the northern hemisphere to practice their craft during their winter season.

---

vineyards and sometimes only in the very best vintages. In Spain, for example, "reserva" indicates the producer has aged the wine longer before its release.

The meaning of reserve seems to vary from country to country and producer to producer and in some cases it has no meaning, so be careful. Read the back label or ask the salesperson for an explanation before spending the extra money.

- **Vielles vignes or old vines** – The older the vine, the lower the yield and often the more concentrated the wine. The actual definition of "old" is sometimes suspect so again check the claim. Vines start to produce at about three years old. A 12-year-old vine is not old; a 100-year-old vine, however, is.

Does a Wine Have to Be Expensive to Be Good?

Ah, the million-dollar question. Sometimes we're asked about the greatest wine we've ever had. One of the best was a '61 Château Lascombes the two of us shared about 10 years ago. Out of a dusty bottle with a label we could hardly read came a wine that will stay in our memories forever. The wine's finish lingered on and on, and still does.

Another one was a bottle of inexpensive Lambrusca shared over chunks of cheese, salami, and plates of pasta when we stopped for lunch at a lorry driver's stop in a small town in Italy one summer. The food and wine combined perfectly in an atmosphere where everyone took the time to enjoy the experience. It, too, was memorable.

The difference in the price of these wines was immense but the value was the same. The enjoyment you derive from a wine may have no relationship to its price. It has more to do with a sense of occasion or sense of place than anything else – who you're with, if you're celebrating anything, the mood you're in, where you are, and what you're eating.

Bottom line, you can find great value, and even memorable wines, at every price point.

WHAT'S IN STORE FOR YOU?

It seems no matter where you buy your wines at retail, most wine displays look the same: sparkling wine in one section, still wines organized by country, and all the really good stuff in a locked glass case. It's predictable, and it's set up for people who already know what they want. As a wine novice, you race in there, find the wine you know, buy it, and race out.

If you are very lucky, you live in an area with a boutique-style shop, with wines organized by style. Looking for an aromatic medium-bodied white wine? Or maybe a concentrated, full-bodied red wine? You walk in and check out the sections that most appeal to you. It's simple, and encourages you to try a wine that's new to you, but in a style you like. If wine shops wanted to sell more wine, or at least be more customer focused, they would all be set up this way.

Service

You should expect the staff of a wine shop to have more knowledge than you, and hopefully have some personal experience with the wines they sell. Can they tell you the difference between a Cabernet Sauvignon from California and one from Chile, for example, and have they actually tasted the wine they are suggesting you buy? Listen to how they describe the wine; it will give you clues as to whether they are knowledgeable or in need of this book.

Will the shop take back wines that have faults? This is very important. It isn't your problem if the wine was not properly made. What if you bought two bottles of the same wine, tried one and didn't like it – can you bring the other one back for an exchange or even full credit? Check the shop's returns policy before you buy from it.

Does the shop have a newsletter? Does it offer in-store tastings? Some shops even offer event planning and glass rentals if you buy the wine through them.

Here are three approaches for getting the wine you want:

- Describe the wine you want in simple terms:
  "I'd like a light-bodied, dry white wine with plenty of acidity for under £6."
  "I prefer red wines that are big and spicy. I usually drink Australian Shiraz and I want to try something different. I want to spend no more than £10."
- Indicate the occasion or the food you plan to serve:
  "We are having pasta with spicy meat sauce tonight. What red wine do you recommend under £5?"
  "I need a special bottle of wine for my anniversary. I'd like to get something really good. I am willing to spend up to £20."
- Ask if they have tasting notes. Better still, ask if you can sample the wine. Don't count on this happening with a £20 wine, but they might open a bottle of something that's being promoted or a special purchase, especially if you are a regular customer.

Selection

Wine selection will differ based on where you live and where you buy your wine. Supermarkets may have better prices or the convenience of being able to buy wine when you nip in for bread, but the staff may be clueless themselves. Plus, you can't be sure if their wines are stored properly.

Wine shops usually have well-trained and helpful staff, but their selection may be in only a narrow range (for example, primarily Italian). You may have to frequent more than one shop to get what you want.

How the shop organizes its selection is important. It should be obvious by looking at the display to determine if the shop has a preference toward one country or another, or wants your business.

Price

There's never any harm in asking for a case discount or lower prices on discontinued wines. Watch for sales or special promotions.

Good Storage – Should You Care?

Wine warehouses can be quite creative in how they merchandise their wines. Some have elaborate shelves and bins and some leave the wine in cardboard boxes on pallets. Some are temperature controlled and others use the door to regulate the temperature in the shop. How they care for the wine is important.

If what you're buying comes from a recently released vintage, the wine won't have been stored long enough to make a difference one way or the other. Just grab a bottle from the shelf or the box on the floor and head to the till.

Make sure any older wine you buy has been stored on its side. Avoid any older wine that has been stored upright. Older wines should be stored in a cool area where they can rest undisturbed.

If it has been stored on its side, check to see that the space between the top of the wine and bottom of the cork (ullage) is not too great, say less than 1 inch (about 2 centimetres). When a wine's been kept upright, or its fill level looks unusually low there's a risk the cork has shrunk and the wine could be oxidized, or at minimum it has prematurely aged.

Never buy any wine that has been stored in a window display. It's been exposed to heat and cold, light and dark.

Ullage

High fill (good)

Low fill (bad)

Wine Shop Do's and Don'ts

Do	Don't
• Buy wine from a shop that has knowledgeable and well-trained staff	• Buy wine from a shop whose staff think all white wine is Chardonnay
• Buy wine from a shop that stores its wine in bins or on racks	• Buy wine from a shop that stores its wine standing up, next to the deli counter
• Buy wine from an outlet that has good stock turnover and is well organized	• Buy wine from a shop where you have to dust the bottles to read the label
• Buy wine from a shop that is temperature controlled	• Buy wine from a shop that uses its door as a temperature-control device
• Buy wine from a place that offers regular tastings and seminars	• Buy wine from a shop that doubles as a general store

VISITING A WINERY

Visiting a winery is not only one of the best ways to buy wine but is also a great way to learn more about wine. You may be able to see how the winery works and even meet the winemaker. Many wineries schedule on-site events during the summer or holiday months – jazz festivals, food tastings, and balloon rides – and some areas hold local wine festivals.

Preparing for a Visit

Before visiting a wine region, it's a good idea to know where you are going, who you are going to visit, and how you are going to cover all the places on your list. Here are some pre-planning suggestions:

- Get a map of the region. Send away to the region's tourist office, wine council or association, or Chamber of Commerce.
- Are there organized tours of the area? If you'd like to take your bike with you, are there trails or is the region bike friendly?
- Do you need to make an appointment? Book ahead and give the winery ample notice of your visit. If you are visiting a wine region on holiday, the place where you are staying may make appointments for you – especially for wineries that rarely see visitors.

   With the exception of certain, larger wineries in France, most European producers prefer an appointment – though the Alsace, the Loire, and Champagne regions encourage visitors. Write a letter, or fax or e-mail in advance of your visit and indicate that you are interested in a tour. We find they are more accommodating if they know you are coming.
- Which wineries have a tasting room and what hours do they keep? While hours may vary according to the season, expect most wineries to be open from 10 AM to 5 PM.

   In Europe, fewer wineries have tasting rooms – you're more than likely to be welcomed in the cellar room itself. The larger producers do offer tours, and some are offered in English.
- Which wineries offer tours of the winery? Don't expect all wineries to offer tours during the harvest season, but if they do it is the best time to take a tour. Tours in the middle of winter can be boring – wine sitting in barrels is less exciting than grapes being crushed and pressed. In our experience, very few wineries charge for tours.
- Does the winery have picnic facilities or a restaurant on the premises? If you are planning a picnic, bring a corkscrew and glasses. Some wineries will oblige you by opening the wine (after you buy it, of course) and providing glasses; however, others have gift shops where they prefer to sell such items.

Planning the Day

While you may think you can visit 20 wineries in a day – and we have seen people try – plan to visit four or five. Two in the morning and three in the afternoon is realistic and allows you to focus on the wine styles you like and to make comparisons among the different styles you try.

Tasting room people are friendlier if you appear attentive and not in a rush. If they see you appreciate their wines, they may let you taste something special.

If a winery offers picnic facilities or has a restaurant, plan to visit it during your trip. There is nothing better than sampling wines with food. Don't forget to make reservations as lots of other people may have the same idea.

Don't just go to the famous wineries. They tend to be overcrowded. You may get a better reception at the smaller wineries and in any case we find they often make more interesting wine.

Allow enough time to drive between wineries. Most are on country roads so it could take more time to travel in the region than you'd expect. It's nice to visit wineries while there are grapes on the vines but be aware that this is also the busiest time to be travelling in wine country.

Assign a designated driver as you will be consuming wine. Better still, hire a driver so everyone can enjoy the event.

At the Winery

One of our best winery experiences was in Burgundy, tasting wines out of the barrel in an ancient cellar with Ghislaine Barthod, the winemaker. The other was with Vincent Arroyo in Calistoga, California, comparing barrel samples of his Petite Sirah from different types of oak. We've toured old châteaux, but also some state-of-the-art facilities, and in all cases we learned so much more about the wine.

Wineries that accept visitors usually have a tasting bar. At the smaller ones, or in Europe, don't be surprised if you end up tasting in the cellar. And if you do end up in the cellar with the winemaker, don't worry if you don't know the local language. You'll be surprised how you can still communicate with gestures and a few simple wine words.

Newer wineries may offer all their wines for tasting, to introduce more people to their products. The more established wineries might have only certain wines available for tasting. Of course, depending on the time of year, smaller wineries may not have any wine left to taste – they have sold out! Late spring, early summer, or during local wine festivals are the safest times to visit if you want to make sure they have wine. Or check ahead if you are concerned about availability.

Sometimes the winery charges for samples. Or they charge for the tasting glass, which usually has their logo etched on it. If you buy wine, this charge is often deducted from the purchase price.

Tasting Etiquette

Here are some suggestions for tasting at a winery:

- Limit your group to four to six people. You will be treated better by the tasting room staff and be able to focus more on the wine. If a crowd is making the trip, call ahead. The winery, if it can handle a large group, may arrange a special tasting just for you.
- Avoid overpowering colognes or perfumes. They will affect your tasting abilities, as well as those of others around you.

- Wineries are providing you with free samples: don't abuse the privilege. Bring bottles of water with you. Don't use wine to quench your thirst.
- Dress appropriately: wine tasting isn't a fashion show. In the New World think casual dress; in the Old World dressy casual. Bring a jumper as some wineries can be cool.
- Pace yourself. The novelty of free wine may have you drinking everything put in front of you. It is okay to spit and you don't need to finish the sample. The people serving at wineries won't be offended if you pour it out, and they will usually have a bucket or spittoon on top of the tasting bar for this purpose. In Europe, follow the lead of the winemaker and spit in the cellar floor drain.
- Don't hog the bar. If there is a crowd and you want to take your time, take your sample and move back to a quieter spot. Let the tasting room staff serve everyone equally. Your questions may be important to you, but other people may just want to taste the wine and move on.
- Thank the staff for their time and the samples of their wine. If you found something you like, buy a couple of bottles to take home.
- Due to the concerns about vine diseases, most wineries prefer you not to walk in the vineyards without permission.

Tasting wine

Use the Four S's and write tasting notes. Wineries sometimes give you their own literature about the wines, but it is always worthwhile to record what you think of the wines. It will help you remember what you tasted when you get home. Besides, it's good practice.

Ask lots of questions – especially if you meet the winemaker. Ask why he or she thinks the wines are unique, what led him or her to winemaking in the first place, or what awards the wines have won. If you want to give feedback on the wine, remember that most winemakers pour their hearts and souls into their wines.

Getting to know a winery and the winemaker adds to the overall appreciation of the wines. A personal connection to the winery always adds to the enjoyment of the wine.

Buying Wine from a Winery

The real benefit of visiting wineries is having a chance to try the wine before you buy. Also, certain wines are available for sale only at the winery. These are usually special wines, in short supply, and are the best bets for buying. Otherwise, why carry around something you can get back home at your local supermarket, unless it is less expensive at the winery? And it often isn't.

You may come across a producer you really like whose wines sell out every year. Get on their mailing list if you want to buy their wines before they sell out. California cult wineries started this trend, and they now allocate who gets their wines, putting them even further out of reach for most people. It's all part of the cachet.

If you're buying a lot of wine, ask for a discount or a bonus bottle (buy 12, get one free). They may be unable to do this due to local laws, but it costs you nothing to ask.

Getting Your Wine Home
Do you want to carry your wine home with you or have it shipped?
Depending on local laws, shipping can be your best bet. Most wineries
are set up to handle mail order shipments. Check this out before you
make the trip. However, make sure your wine doesn't arrive home before
you do.

At times when shipping isn't practical, plan ahead and carry a cooler to
protect your wine purchases, especially during the summer months.
Extreme prolonged heat will shorten the lifespan of some wines, and even
after a few hours in a locked car the cork could be forced out of the bottle.

Shipping wine home from overseas is very costly. On top of the
shipping costs, expect to pay duties, taxes, markups, brokerage, and
handling fees. Your £6 wine could end up costing another £10 a bottle
just to get it into the country. Check local availability before you decide
to buy abroad.

Be selective about what you buy and carry it home if at all possible.
You will save the shipping, brokerage, and handling fees. A standard-
sized wine bottle weighs about 2 lb (1 kg) and is sturdy enough to travel
well in your carry-on luggage. (We've tested it out in the interest of wine
travellers everywhere.) We have seen other people check their wine on
planes in unprotected cartons – not a good idea!

Check your duty-free allowance and be prepared to pay tax and duty
for anything above those limits. It is also possible to declare wine that
isn't accompanying you on the trip. You may be able to save some extra
duties this way.

BUYING OVER THE INTERNET

In the event that you don't have enough places to buy wine locally, or if
you live in a remote area where the only wine on the shelves has the
word "hearty" somewhere on the label, then the Internet may be the
place for you. Like any purchase over the Internet, the choices may be
great but there are many cautionary tales to consider. It is one thing to
have a book shipped to you in January, another thing to have a case of
wine rattling around in the back of a delivery van.

There Are Rules

Assuming your area has no restrictions on buying wine from a website
and, more importantly, having it shipped to you, how do you go about
it? The first step is to set up an account. You will be required to provide
personal information such as date of birth and credit card information to
pre-qualify you as a buyer. Website retailers must ensure that they're not
selling alcohol to a minor, so some request a fax copy of your driving
licence, passport, or official ID before anything is sold or shipped to you.

Buyer Beware

Once the paperwork is in place, you can browse the site as you would
any other site, choosing what you want to add to your shopping cart.
Then you check out and pay. Seems simple, doesn't it?

Maybe, but there are certain extra precautions to take when buying wine this way. Wine, at its most basic, is food. It has a shelf life. If subjected to extremes of heat or cold, or poor storage conditions, it will spoil. This means you need to know at least two things about the Internet retailer: how does it *store* and how does it *ship* its wine?

Before you place an order, do a little research into how the Internet wine retailer operates. Explore the sites, look into its buying, storage, and shipping policies, and ask questions of the staff by e-mail. Once you're satisfied with what you've seen and heard, place a small order as a trial run.

Shipping the Wine

The responsibility for and cost of shipping arrangements generally rest with the buyer. When you make these arrangements, consider the time in transit (is it days or weeks?) and the prevailing weather conditions. One Internet retailer has a link to the Weather Channel so buyers can decide on the best time to place an order for shipment.

Even if you can't or don't want to order wines through a website, many are great resources or gateways to other wine-related sites.

BUYING AT AN AUCTION

Auctions can be dangerous to your bank account. Often the excitement of the auction relieves you of all logic; on the other hand, it allows you to acquire wine you otherwise wouldn't be able to get at a local shop.

Why Buy at an Auction?

Auctions give you access to wines that have long since sold out at the retail level – special vintages, unique bottles, or hard-to-find producers. You may want these to celebrate a special birthday, an anniversary, or some other milestone event.

The wines you'll see featured at an auction tend to be rarities and keepers – wines that are special in some way because they are of limited availability and have demonstrated longevity. Don't expect to find bargains or a £5 everyday wine for your next party.

Types of Auctions

The most common types of wine auctions in your area will be either commercial (live and via the Internet), estate, or for a charitable cause. Commercial and charity auctions can be large scale, with hundreds of lots (the bottles or cases of wine for sale) to bid on. We've seen lots as small as one bottle, and as large as a 20-year vertical (a successive series of vintages of one wine) of Château Mouton-Rothschild.

Different types of auctions have different fees or *premiums* attached to them. Check in advance to see if there are any hidden costs.

Preparing for an Auction

Do your homework. All auction wines are sold "as is." You assume all risk once your bid has been accepted. Request an auction catalogue, which will be free or at a nominal charge. In it you will find descriptions of the wines up for bid, with quotes from internationally recognized wine experts who have tasted these wines before.

Auction wines are appraised. There is usually an estimated per bottle price provided, and sometimes a reserve price, a minimum below which the lot won't be sold. A recent online auction listed a 1799 Château Lafite-Rothschild with "Please enquire" next to the estimated per bottle price. This bottle could sell for £10,000.

Use the catalogue to do some research on local availability and price. That way you won't find out later that the two bottles you just bought for £100 were also available at Joe's Wine Warehouse for £50.

The catalogue description also gives you clues to a wine's condition before you bid – in particular, the level of wine in the bottle. As wine ages, the fill level gradually decreases. Level is measured as the gap between the top of the wine and the bottom of the cork, otherwise known as *ullage* (see also p 141). A low fill level means some of the wine has leaked out or evaporated, or both, and may mean the wine has oxidized. Low fill levels are to be expected with very old bottles of wine.

If you've done your homework and want to participate, you'll have to register for the auction.

Ullage Levels

High fill	Normal fill	Mid-shoulder	Low-shoulder
Excellent	Good news!	Start to worry	Bad

At the Auction

The bidding at an auction tends to go very quickly. The auctioneer typically sets the level of the first bid, and bidders jump in from there. You'll have a numbered paddle to flash if you are interested in raising the price.

As we said earlier, don't get carried away in the heat of the moment. If price levels get beyond your limits, let the lot go. You will have many more opportunities to find wines from the best years at other auctions.

WINE-BUYING CLUBS

Wine clubs offer members a chance to buy wines not otherwise available through regular channels. They might also organize private wine-tasting events, where you'll get a chance to taste, and possibly buy, unique wines and to meet fellow wine enthusiasts.

Most clubs require a one-time enrolment fee and annual subscription. You should weigh this against the selection of wines offered and the convenience of the club. Does the club require you to buy a certain amount of wine each year to remain an active member? Does it offer adequate descriptions of the wine it is selling? It's a good idea to check out how the club delivers its wines to you and how long it will take.

One limitation of many wine clubs is having to buy wine in case quantities: either six or 12 bottles. You either have to really like what you're buying, or find someone else in the group who's willing to trade some of what they bought for some of what you bought.

Wine-of-the-month clubs run by a winery or a wine retailer – where every month you receive a package of wines chosen by them – may seem like a good idea but you often have little or no say in the selection. It's one way to try new wines but not the best. On the other hand, if you live in an isolated area it may be the only option you have. Getting a surprise package every month from a winery you like, however, will be something of a treat.

WILL AUNT MABEL LIKE THE TROCKENBEERENAUSLESE?

Wine and wine-related items make excellent gifts. They can be given to acknowledge someone, or to mark a special occasion, as long as you're sure there are no health, cultural, or religious reasons to avoid them. Even if you don't know the recipient very well, think back to whether you've ever seen the person drink wine, or express an interest in it.

Wine doesn't have to be expensive to be a successful gift. Following are some reasons for giving the gift of wine, along with suggestions.

Trockenbeerenauslese
If you can track down a bottle of this highly prized dessert wine, it will make a special gift for anyone on your list. If Aunt Mabel has great taste, she'll love it!

Acknowledging Someone

You may want to use wine as a reward or to acknowledge some special contribution someone has made. Choose something that is less well known, or has personal meaning or a story to tell. Consider giving wine from a winery you visited, specially selected to go along with a person's favourite food, or made by a winemaker who is "one to watch."

Beyond what's in the bottle, think about packaging and presentation. Non-standard bottles – small and large – are often attractively packaged for gift giving. Make sure the wine inside is good too.

If you are considering a large-volume wine purchase, and you live near a wine region, you may be able to get personalized labels printed up. Many wineries don't label their wines until they're ready to sell, and would be willing to customize a label for you.

Moving up the price scale, you can always count on name recognition with wine from a well-known producer: Château Mouton-Rothschild in Bordeaux, or the super-Tuscan Sassicaia from Italy, for example. Now, you might think these are safer bets, but if too expensive they may be inappropriate for the occasion.

For Special Occasions

Birthdays and anniversaries are easy when it comes to wine. For a start, you have the birth year or anniversary year to match with a vintage. Of course, this assumes the birthday person isn't sensitive about sharing his or her exact age.

Finding a birth-year wine for someone who is going to be 40 years old next week is going to be difficult, and expensive, so you could make it very easy for yourself by planning years in advance. But how many wines age successfully for 10, 20, or more years? You'll have to consider both the wine itself and its vintage. Bordeaux red wines, for example, are renowned for longevity, but whether they peak at 10 or 35 years will depend on the vintage. Usually only the better, more expensive wines, will last 20 or more years.

Not many New World wines have established the track record that the Old World has; however, some think the 1995 California Cabernet Sauvignons will age well.

Sweet wines, especially those with good acidity, are also safe bets, as are fortified wines like port and Madeira. Port – in particular the 1997 vintage – is the safest bet. Even the best versions are not nearly as expensive as top Bordeaux, yet will appreciate in value as they age. You can buy the '97 port now when your niece is three years old, and give it to her for her 21st birthday.

Here are a few options for wines that are available and will likely age well for up to 25 years:

White wines	Red Wines	Fortified
Sauternes	Bordeaux cru	Vintage ports
German Rieslings –	Barolo	Madeira
Beerenauslese, Eiswein, or	Northern Rhône (Syrah)	
Trockenbeerenauslese	California Cabernet Sauvignon	

Now that you know which ones to look for, there's the vintage to consider. Actually, this is relatively easy to find out. Wines from bad vintages will have been consumed long ago, and ones from good vintages may still be kicking around in auctions. You're in luck if you're looking for a gift for someone born in 1945. That was a fabulous vintage for both Bordeaux and Sauternes wines, and they're still available for sale – if money is no object.

What about other occasions? Here are some ideas:

Occasion	Wine
Valentine's Day	St. Amour Beaujolais
Wedding gift	Vintage champagne
Baby's birth	Vintage port
First job	Cava
Promotion	Non-vintage champagne
Christmas	Zinfandel
Housewarming	Chianti Classico

 The most immediately gratifying special-occasion wine gift is sparkling wine. A perfect wine to celebrate anything!

Bringing Wine to a Dinner Party

When bringing wine to a dinner party, keep in mind the following:

- Don't expect that the wine you bring will be consumed that evening. Your host may have other plans. Don't expect that it won't be consumed, either.
- It's a good idea to contact the host in advance if you would like to bring along something appropriate to that evening's menu. If he or she is open to the idea, see whether the wine you had in mind works with the planned menu. Or if the menu is a surprise and the host wants you to bring a surprise wine, consider these food-friendly wines:

White wines	Red Wines
Riesling, Sauvignon Blanc, or Chenin Blanc	Pinot Noir, Chianti, Barbera, or Rioja

- Even if your host has selected wines to accompany the meal, ask about bringing something for before or after – an apéritif wine to stimulate the appetite, or a dessert wine for afterward. Here are some great ideas to try:

To Start	To Finish
Sparkling wine (Prosecco or Cava) Dry sherry (Amontillado, dry Oloroso) Muscadet, Vinho Verde	Late harvest Riesling Tokaji from Hungary Port (ruby or tawny)

How Much Is Enough?
The general rule of thumb is one-half bottle (three glasses – one white and two red) of wine per person for dinner. If the guests are staying over you may want to increase this slightly. Take into account the designated drivers, and scale back the quantities if the guest list includes teetotalers.

WINE-RELATED GIFTS

Wine is a great gift; ideally, it will leave the recipient with an experience to remember. But when it's gone, it's gone. For those times when you want to give something more durable, wine-related accessories may fit the bill.

Books

Here are some books that make our short list:

- **For the traveller** – Hugh Johnson and Jancis Robinson's *World Atlas of Wine*, Fifth Edition, is an indispensable guide for someone planning (or dreaming about) a wine-focused holiday.

- **For budding wine pros** – Michael Schuster's *Essential Winetasting* and Andrew Sharp's *Winetaster's Secrets* are great gifts.
- **For the serious wine lover** – The pinnacle of wine books is Jancis Robinson's *Oxford Companion to Wine*, Second Edition, which any wine enthusiast would love to have. There is a version specific to North America, as well as a shorter *Companion* version.
- **For the net surfer** – *The Good Web Guide* leads you straight to the best wine sites.

Videos

To better understand wine, try the video series by Jancis Robinson or the one by Hugh Johnson.

Magazine Subscriptions

For those who like to stay current on what's happening in the wine world, a magazine subscription can be a great gift. Besides the news and the articles, most wine magazines contain reviews of recently released wines. If the recipient likes to buy wine, choose the magazine that best represents what's available in his or her home market.

- *Wine Spectator*, *Wine & Spirits*, and *Wine Enthusiast* have a distinctly U.S. perspective.

- *The Vine* is a subscription-only fine wine magazine. www.clive-coates.co.uk

- *Decanter* and *Wine* are published in the U.K.

Newsletters

A number of wine writers publish regular monthly newsletters that can be given as a gift subscription. For example, Robert Parker Jr. publishes *The Wine Advocate* – probably the most influential, if not controversial, newsletter in North America. Many write only for their local wine market and are more appropriate for people who want to know what's available closer to home.

Tools and Toys

Earlier we talked about three corkscrews that work very well. Either the Screwpull style or the Waiter's Friend style would make good gifts. They are available in different colours and finishes, and can be engraved.

If you want to give someone something really special, the Laguiole handmade corkscrew is the waiter's *real* friend. We won't mention the corkscrew you fit on a counter that lets you open a bottle every two seconds or the other Screwpull that costs about £45. Give them wine to go with the less expensive and more practical corkscrew – they'll appreciate it.

An even more practical gift is a wine preserver system like Vacu-Vin or Epivac or the inert gas Private Preserve. This assumes that your friend has bottles of wine left over to preserve.

Glassware and Decanters

From the all-purpose tulip shape to extreme customized glass shapes, there's something for everyone. Would they appreciate a glass specifically designed to enhance the taste of Chianti, for example?

Decanters are another option, especially if the recipient enjoys young red wines that need aeration, or older wines or port that have sediment.

Thinking outside the Box

Think chillers (in marble or terra cotta, or freezable ones), pewter bottle stoppers, decanting funnels and coasters, glass aerating funnels, wine racks, wine tags to identify bottles in the cellar, and, even, red wine stain remover.

Online Retailers

www.bbr.co.uk
www.bordeauxdirect.com
www.amazon.co.uk
www.oddbins.com
www.sundaytimeswineclub.co.uk
www.enjoyment.co.uk

For the real wine snob, consider Nez de Vin. This is a kit to help the taster learn to identify the hundreds of aromas contained in wine.

And if money is no object, try a wine cellar. Essentially wine fridges, they hold from fifty to over a thousand bottles in a temperature- and humidity-controlled environment.

MINE, ALL MINE

WHY KEEP WINE?

It's been said that most wines are consumed within 36 hours of purchase, so why have your own collection? For convenience, variety, because some wines taste better with time, and because you'll save money.

Once you have a few bottles of your favourite wines on hand, all you need to do is walk over to your cupboard or down to your basement and grab something out of your "cellar."

It's also been said that most of the world's wines are produced to be consumed within a few years of the vintage, so only a small proportion are worthy of cellaring. It's one thing to have a few wines ageing nicely in your basement, but it is another thing to know *when* to drink them. We'll try to help you out with that, too.

We're not going to talk about collecting for investment purposes. While wine is considered by some to be a good financial investment, it is our opinion that wine is to be enjoyed – either soon after purchase or following some much-needed rest in cellarland.

WHAT SHOULD WE HAVE TONIGHT?

One of the simplest reasons for having a cellar is convenience. Just like a restaurant with a chalkboard wine list, you too can have a supply of ready-to-drink wines available by the bottle, or even by the glass. You can try out different wines with what you're serving, and see which ones work best. Any partial bottles can be sealed up for another time using your vacuum hand pump or inert gas.

If you haven't developed any personal favourites yet, it's a good idea, and a lot of fun, to experiment with different varieties, regions, and producers. This way you'll be able to try wines within a range of styles and flavours. Just don't buy a lot of one wine.

If you are lucky enough to have a good wine shop nearby, don't worry about keeping more than a few everyday wines on hand. Let the shop be your wine storage location and save your money for longer-term keepers.

If you don't have a good shop nearby, or would prefer to do your wine shopping less frequently, then you need to do some planning. Based on the style of wine you like, your eating habits, the space you have, and of course your wine-drinking habits, there should be something for everyone. The key is to buy versatile, food-friendly wines that will appeal to a variety of tastes.

> *Time Sensitive*
> Buy two bottles of the same wine. Drink one right away and save the other one for six months to a year. Keep notes of when you tasted the first wine and discover how the wine evolved with time in the bottle. Not recommended for Beaujolais Nouveau.

Wine Staples

 Remember, most of the wines you will be buying are for short-term storing – we call them your wine staples – and the vintages are whatever the shop has available to sell. We'll leave prices up to you, but versions of these wines usually cost under £10. You can go for a variety of wines or just some basics – your choice.

Variety pack
Keep a case on hand of the following wines. One bottle of each should do it:

- Reds: Chianti, Barbera, Dolcetto, Beaujolais, Merlot, Côtes du Rhône-Villages, Pinot Noir
- Whites: Unoaked Chardonnay, Riesling, Sauvignon Blanc
- Other: Cava, Rosé

Basics pack
Another option is to double up on some of the more versatile varietals. Here's what a case could look like:

- Reds: Chianti (2), Pinot Noir (2), Merlot
- Whites: Oaked Chardonnay, Unoaked Chardonnay, Sauvignon Blanc (2), Riesling (2)
- Other: Cava

Top Seven

If you want to buy the wines that are made from the Top Seven grapes, here are some options, ranging from the classics to regions where you'll probably get a good deal.

What to buy

Wine	Classic Regions	Regions to Explore	Value Regions
Chardonnay	Burgundy (France) United States	Spain Italy	Chile
Sauvignon Blanc	Loire (France) Bordeaux (France) New Zealand	South Africa	Entre-Deux-Mers (Bordeaux)
Riesling	Germany Alsace (France)	South Australia	
Cabernet Sauvignon	Bordeaux (France)	Chile	Eastern Europe
Merlot	Bordeaux (France) Italy	Chile Languedoc (France)	Chile
Pinot Noir	Burgundy (France)	New Zealand Oregon California	
Syrah/Shiraz	Rhône (France) Australia	Argentina Languedoc (France) South Africa United States	Fitou or Minervois (Vins de Pays d'Oc)

> *Wine Myth*
> Not all wines benefit from ageing. In fact, less than 10% of all wines
> produced benefit from more than two years of ageing.

BUYING FOR THE FUTURE

So you got yourself a subscription to *Wine or Decanter* and now you
want to buy some of those big, tannic wines you've been reading about.
You've read they need a few years cellaring time before they are
drinkable. When you checked to see if any of the 1990 Brunellos that are
"drinking nicely" are in your wine shop, you were surprised to see them
selling for more than double the price of the current vintage. It's time to
start buying now and holding for the future. What to do?

The three things you need to consider are the kind of wines you
like, what you're willing to spend on something you can't drink for a
few years, and how many wines you can store under the proper
conditions.

Which Wines Age?

If you drink only light-bodied white wines or rosé wines, this section
isn't for you. These wines don't improve with age and in fact will start to
lose their fresh fruit aromas and flavours with cellaring. The same applies
for most light-bodied red wines; however, a year in a cellar won't hurt
them as much.

If you prefer full-bodied, sweet, or fortified wines, then
longer-term cellaring of these wines is a good option. Sufficient
acid and/or tannins are the essential components that allow
wines to age. If a wine has the potential to age, you can buy what you can
afford now, while prices are low, and keep it until the tannins in the wine
have softened when it's at its prime. Only very good wines have any
flavour left when this happens.

The following grape varieties tend to age well. Some other grape
varieties (for example, Sémillon, Sauvignon Blanc, Chardonnay, and
Sangiovese) are candidates for long cellaring but usually only when
associated with certain wines.

White Grape Varieties	Red Grape Varieties
Riesling	Cabernet Sauvignon
Chenin Blanc	Syrah
Furmint	Nebbiolo

Good wines have more of the components that allow them to age
properly than average wines. If you are looking for specific wines, here
are some options for medium-term cellaring of up to five years:

White Wines	Red Wines
Burgundy – grand cru	Bordeaux – top grand cru classé
German Riesling –	Burgundy – grand cru
Auslese and up	Northern Rhône
Alsace – Vendage Tardive	Barolo
Pessac-Léognan	Brunello di Montalcino
Vouvray – moelleux	Chianti Classico riserva
Sauternes and Barsac	Super-Tuscans
Tokaji	California Cabernet (top wines)
	Australian Shiraz (top wines)
	Vintage champagne – prestige
	cuvées
	Vintage port
	Madeira

If you have the space, and the budget, these candidates are ideal for even longer-term cellaring:

White Wines	Red Wines
Burgundy – premier cru	Bordeaux – cru bourgeois and
Chablis	lesser cru classé
California Chardonnay	Burgundy – premier cru
German Riesling – Auslese	Châteauneuf-du-Pape
Alsace Riesling and	Chianti Classico
Gewürztraminer	Vino Nobile di Montepulciano
Graves	Rioja reserva
Hunter Valley Semillon	Ribera del Duero
Canadian icewine	New World Cabernet Sauvignon
Monbazillac	New World Pinot Noir
	Australian Shiraz
	Zinfandel

Here's what you may be able to expect from certain wines if you wait long enough:

- Burgundies in exceptional years are at their best in 15 or more years.
- Bordeaux in exceptional years can last over 20 years.
- Top Barolos and Brunello di Montalcinos in exceptional years can last 20 to 25 years.
- Vintage port can last 40 or more years.
- Malmsey Madeira has been known to last over 100 years.
- And a few Tokaji Essencia have even made it to 200 years.

Sometimes a great winemaker can perform miracles in a bad vintage, but the only way to know this is to read wine magazines. Almost everyone else relies on vintage charts.

Vintages

Certain vintages, in certain regions, are better than others for cellaring.

For red wines, tannins help wines age. In dry years, the grape skins are thicker and therefore contribute more tannins. In vintages where there is more rain, there is more pulp and the skins are thinner – the wines are more dilute and won't age as well.

For white wine, acidity is important. In cooler years, acidity levels are higher and the grapes will age better. But in both cases, the grapes must still be sufficiently ripe so that there is enough flavour (extract) in the wine for it to age properly.

Bottle sizes

Oxygen speeds the ageing process of wine. Once a wine gets into the bottle it is exposed only to the small amount of oxygen at the top of the bottle, called the *headspace*. Once the wine has used that up, the process of ageing becomes reductive – which is much slower and better than oxidative. The amount of headspace is more or less the same for all sizes of bottles. It would stand to reason then that larger-format bottles – like magnums – have less oxygen relative to their volume of wine than much smaller half bottles. Small bottles, therefore, age faster than large bottles. How much faster is anyone's guess, but most collectors bet on the large-format bottles for serious ageing.

DO YOU HAVE TO SPEND MUCH?

Wines for longer-term cellaring don't have to be expensive. We started to put wines away about 15 years ago after reading an article called something like "Ten Wines under £5 That Will Taste Like £10 Wines in Five Years." We bought two bottles each of the recommended wines and stored them, lying on their sides, in a couple of old shelving units in a cool place in our basement.

We started enjoying the wines over time and finished the last one in our starter pack after about seven years of cellaring. This convinced us of the benefit of buying ageworthy wines we liked, because they did improve in the bottle.

Although we saved a bit of money (because the current vintage of the wines had increased in price), these aged wines, based on how they had evolved, were actually more like wines that cost double the price. So your cellar does not have to be full of super-Tuscan wines. Just buy wines that you like and can afford, in good vintages, that will improve over time.

What about a cellar, does it have to cost a lot of money to build? Not at all. In fact, you may not even have to build anything. A wine cellar can be as simple as a few wooden boxes in the back corner of a dark cupboard, or an old bookcase, or some inexpensive shelves. At the other extreme, your cellar can be a temperature-controlled room with redwood racking and track lighting in the basement of your house.

It all depends, do you want to spend your money on wine or on storage? As long as you keep your wine away from its true enemies – heat, light, and vibration – a wine cellar can cost you next to nothing.

THE RIGHT CONDITIONS

Here's all your wine needs when you store it for any length of time: constant temperature, darkness, humidity, clean environment with good ventilation, and lastly, peace and quiet.

Constant Temperature

The most important factor in wine storage is maintaining a constant temperature. Temperature fluctuations – even 5°F (2–3°C) over the course of the day – are detrimental to wines.

Find an area where the temperature is within the range of 50–60°F (10–15°C), and where temperatures don't vary on a daily basis. A variation of about 10°F (4–5°C) between summer and winter is fine as long as the shift is gradual. The ideal temperature is 55°F (13°C).

If you don't live in a château in France, it may be difficult to achieve this temperature range. If your wine rack catches the evening sun, or the broom cupboard where you store your wines has the water heater in it, try to move your wines to where the temperature is at least constant. See if you can insulate the area in some way, but not with fibreglass insulation, as it absorbs moisture. And if there is nothing you can do, don't worry, even a constant 70°F (20°C) isn't going to ruin your wines – maybe just knock a year or so off their development.

But if the temperature where you store your wines fluctuates dramatically, or you are getting serious about collecting wine, you may have to give in and buy a temperature-controlled unit.

Darkness

Wine likes to be kept in the dark. Direct sunlight not only increases the temperature of the wine, but also the UV rays penetrate the bottle and harm the wine. The dark green glass used for most wines doesn't completely protect the contents.

Don't store wines near a fluorescent light source either. Whether you use the corner of a dark cupboard or something bigger, don't have any more light than you need to move around and retrieve wines. Even a bare incandescent light bulb left on will give off heat.

Humidity

A high, constant level of humidity will save corks and protect your wine. Anything within the range of 60–80% humidity is fine, with the ideal level being 70–75%. Humidity is most important when you plan to store bottles for more than five years.

Below the 50% mark, corks will dry out, start to leak, and the wine will oxidize. Above the 80% level, mould will form and labels will get damaged and may fall off. Given the choice between low and high humidity environments, think, is it better to ruin my wine or my labels?

A quick fix is to keep an opened jug of water on the floor where you store your wines. If this doesn't work, the need for controlled humidity is in order. Temperature-controlled units also take care of humidity.

Swell Corks

If you don't know the level of humidity in your house, you can buy an inexpensive hygrometer, with a digital readout. It is a fairly accurate device and will give you a sense of what you may need to adjust.

Clean and Well Ventilated

Clean means odour free. Don't keep your wines near laundry detergents, paints, fertilizers, or other chemicals. That goes for anything smelly, including cooking odours or gym equipment.

Remember, wine breathes. Slowly, over time, minute amounts of air pass through the cork, making contact with the wine. You don't want your wine to remind you of the garlic you stored in the cellar three years ago, do you?

The same goes for cardboard boxes. If the storage area is humid, the cardboard will start to rot and may contaminate your wine. Ask your local wine shop if they will give or sell you any of the wooden wine crates the more expensive wines are shipped in.

As for ventilation, does the air circulate where your wine is being kept? Or is it too drafty? A racking system helps the air circulate and is better for long-term storage than sealed boxes.

Show and Tell

If you have accumulated a few hundred wines and want to control temperature and humidity, you can purchase a self-contained, temperature-controlled unit that you can plug into any electrical outlet. These are usually wood veneered and feature a glass window so you can see your prized collection. Prices start at about £300 for a 200-bottle capacity and go up to a few thousand for walk-in units.

Peace and Quiet

Think of your wines as "sleeping" in the cellar. If they don't get their sleep, they won't evolve properly and will age prematurely.

Make sure you keep them in an area that is free from vibration. Keep them away from the washing machine and the fridge. Resist the temptation of picking up your bottles every two to three months and looking at them. Nothing has changed, trust us.

Try to dedicate one area for wine storage. Having to move your wines frequently isn't good for them, or your back.

Keep away from the Fridge!

The only place worse than storing your wines in the fridge is on a wine rack on top of the fridge. It might look pretty, and you don't use the space, but vibrations, temperature, and light fluctuations will prematurely age your wines.

And while it's dark inside the fridge, the temperature is too cold and the humidity too low for long-term storage. The vibrations from the motor cycling on and off will also harm the wine eventually.

WHAT ABOUT SHELVING?

The key thing about shelving or racking isn't what its made of, but that it allows the bottles to lie horizontal – not standing up. Otherwise, the corks will dry out.

Crates may be fine in the short term, but eventually, you'll get tired of finding that the wine you want is always at the bottom of the crate. When you are ready to set up some shelving to organize your collection, here are some options:

- Use an old bookcase.
- Put a few simple shelves together. Make sure they're solid. Square clay chimney pipes work well if you have the space.
- Inexpensive pine shelves designed for wine bottles are relatively easy to get.
- Wine supply stores sell premade wine racks in various styles and sizes. Racks that have a space for each bottle are more expensive than ones that hold six to eight bottles per section. You can usually mix and match these systems for look and convenience.
- Hire professionals to custom build racking for your storage space. Use redwood if it's available. It's strong, resistant to moisture, and doesn't give off odours that could taint the wine.

The key points to remember when planning your wine storage space are:

- **Circulation** – Can air circulate around the bottles?
- **Flexibility** – Can bottles with larger bases (e.g., champagne), half bottles, and large bottle formats (e.g., magnums) fit in the racking? How easy is it to add on to the shelving if you want to expand your collection?
- **Space** – Always plan for more space than you think you'll need!

When planning a storage space, think ahead. If you are planning on moving in the foreseeable future, limit the size of your collection. Like all those books you've also been collecting, wine is heavy and cumbersome. You might not think 200 wines is a lot, but that's 17 cases, or half a pallet of wine!

IT'S ALL ABOUT BALANCE

The kinds of wines and number of bottles you decide to keep in your cellar will depend on your budget and your motivation for having a cellar. Ultimately, it's about balance. What's inside your cellar should strike a balance between immediate enjoyment and future appreciation.

In the beginning, your wine budget may cover only less expensive wines, most of which will be suited for immediate consumption, plus a few that are capable of improving with time.

The balance will start to shift as the wines you originally put aside for long-term cellaring start to mature, and become your "drink now" wines. These get replaced with more wines to lay down for the future. Over time, you'll need to buy fewer and fewer wines for your current needs.

Organizing Your Wines

A dozen of so bottles isn't too hard to keep track of, but as you add to your collection, you'll need a system. It's never a pleasant surprise to discover a couple of bottles of five-year-old Beaujolais Nouveau tucked away in a crate somewhere. You don't want to lose track of the wines that don't improve with age. You need to know their whereabouts at all times.

The simplest system you can set up is based on a logbook. In it, list your wines, their prices, short notes from wine write-ups, and whether they are "drink now" or "keepers." For keepers, indicate in bold letters the year you were told the wine would be "drinking nicely."

As you drink each wine, add your tasting notes, including who you shared the wine with, and what was on the menu. If you have multiple bottles of the same wine, highlight whether the wine was great (at its peak), needed time (too young), or was starting to fade (overmature). Plan a party if you have a few bottles in that last category!

If you want to put your wine list on the computer, you can do it yourself or buy cellar management software. We've gone the DIY route and have our wine list on a spreadsheet. A database programme would work fine too, but they weren't very user-friendly when we first set up our system 12 years ago. The different fields we use are year, wine type, producer, tasting notes, and last known price. This system is good if you like poring over your wine list, sometimes exclaiming, "Hey, I forgot we had that one!"

The beauty of cellar management software is it allows you to look at your wines from a variety of perspectives. You can see whether you have different years of the same wine, which wines are ready to drink now, and which wine and food matches would work best. If you're already using a spreadsheet or database, you can easily import the information. Most software programmes also allow you to download cellaring guidelines and tasting notes for your wines from the Internet. Some also have search capabilities so you can find certain wine styles quickly.

Buy a Couple or a Case?

Start by buying your wines in one-, two-, or three-bottle increments. Don't even think about purchasing a case of one wine when you first start your cellar unless you are very sure you like the wine. You'll have a great deal of money tied up in one type of wine, and as your tastes evolve, you might not like it as much as when you first bought it.

Even if you do like the wine, why narrow your options? This summer, one of us fell in love with a nice Moscato d'Asti, and got carried away and bought a case. It's a great little wine, but it doesn't keep and our friends didn't like it as much as we did. The prospect of having to drink the same wine every week for the rest of the summer wasn't too appealing. Luckily, we were able to exchange half the case for something else.

SAMPLE CELLARS

Below is a menu of wine choices based on wine styles. Wines in the "Near Future" column are wines for mid-term storage. Wines in the "Hold" column are for longer-term storage. Wines you purchase for long-term storage should be from good to excellent vintages and from good, reliable producers.

	Drink Now	Near Future	Hold
Under £10	Light-bodied whites Light-bodied reds Sparkling	Medium-bodied reds	
£10 to £20	Rosé Sherry Medium-bodied whites Sparkling wines	Late harvest dessert Full-bodied whites	Select late harvest Dessert
Over £20	NV champagne	Vintage champagne	Full-bodied whites Full-bodied reds Dessert (e.g., icewine) Vintage port Madeira

BUILDING FOR THE FUTURE

How much wine do you need? And how much space do you need to allow for your cellar? Here are some calculations that might be useful:

To have a cellar doesn't mean you need to rush out and buy 10 years worth of wine today. You can build toward the goal of a perpetual cellar, with wines that are going to be consumed in the short-term, as well as long-term keepers. Always buy wine to replace what you drink plus a few for longer-term storage.

If you drink:	Include extras for gifts, etc.	Annual consumption	Need for short-term consumption (2 years)	Need for long-term consumption (10 years)
1 bottle/wk	1 bottle/mth	64 bottles	128 bottles (11 cases)	640 bottles (53 cases)
2 bottles/wk	1 bottle/mth	116 bottles	232 bottles (19 cases)	1,160 bottles (97 cases)
5 bottles/wk	4 bottle/mth	308 bottles	616 bottles (51 cases)	3,080 bottles (257 cases)

DOES WINE IMPROVE INDEFINITELY?

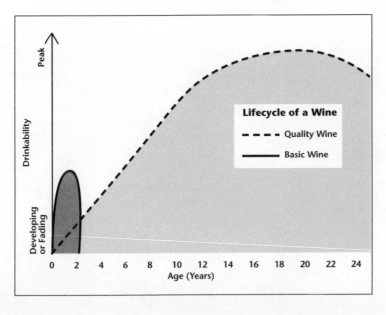In a word, no. The life cycle of wine can be short and sweet, or can be long and fruitful. Wines have to have that rare balance of fruit, acidity, and tannins to make it over the long haul. But even wines with that rare balance will eventually decline.

As you taste more and more wine, you will begin to notice the difference between young and mature wines. With more practice, you will notice that some wines seem to need more time, while others will have reached their peak or a plateau, or at some point declined. When to drink a wine is a matter of personal taste and only you can decide what you like.

> ***We Will Drink Wine Before Its Time***
> Up until the 1980s, wines were made for ageing – 10 to 15 years or more – but nowadays the trend is toward making softer, fruitier wines that can be consumed right away or with only three to five years of ageing.

It helps to have some idea of when your wine will be ready to drink. Ask the sales assistant or do some research on your own. There are many books and websites that provide this information. Contact the winery directly if you are really interested, though we generally find that wineries seem to think their wines will last twice as long as they actually do. Keep track of the "drink by" date in your logbook, or if you have cellar management software, this information should be part of the regular updates.

Fortunately, the window for drinking wine at its best is wide, usually months or even years, so you won't need to be home on May 9, 2005, to drink that nice bottle of Brunello you just bought.

As a general rule, it's better to drink a wine early, when it still has life in it, than to hang on too long and drink it past its prime.

Is My Bottle of '56 Bordeaux Ready Yet?

We are often asked questions like this, and unfortunately it requires a somewhat complex answer. It depends on the wine's vintage, the producer, how it was made, and how and where it was stored.

It's been said, "There are no great wines, only great bottles of wine." Although a single bottle of wine has much in common with others of the same vintage, once it leaves the winery it is subject to the care and handling of many different people until it reaches you.

May the wine you drink have been cared for in every stage of its journey from the vineyard to your table.

INDEX

NOTES

NOTES

NOTES

NOTES